EVEREST CALLING

XC 30

Everest

Ascent of the Dark Side:

Calling

The Mallory-Irvine Ridge

Lorna Siggins

MAINSTREAM
PUBLISHING

First published in Great Britain in 1994 by
MAINSTREAM PUBLISHING COMPANY
(EDINBURGH) LTD
7 Albany Street
Edinburgh EH1 3UG

ISBN 1 85158 663 6

A catalogue record for this book is available from the
British Library

Designed by James Hutcheson

Typeset in Adobe Garamond by Litho Link Ltd,
Welshpool, Powys, Wales

Printed in Spain by AGT
D.L.TO:931-1994

PREVIOUS PAGE:

SUNSET ON THE NORTH COL. PUMORI ON THE LEFT, CHO OYU TO ITS RIGHT. (JM)

❋ *Contents* ❋

❈ *Acknowledgments* ❈

The Irish Everest Expedition climbed the mountain, the Irish Himalayan Trust has initiated this book. Without the support of *The Irish Times*, it would never have got past the first full stop.

I owe an immeasurable debt to Dermot Somers, climber, writer and expedition diarist; to John Bourke, who co-ordinated the whole effort; and to Jonathan Williams, Don Roberts, Rose Doyle, John Murray and Judy Diamond – agent, advisor(s), film-maker and editor, respectively. I am grateful for the references provided by Joss Lynam, Audrey Salkeld, Xavier Eguskitza, Dr John de Courcy Ireland, and the Tibet Support Group-Ireland.

The right words of encouragement at the right time came from colleagues in *The Irish Times*, principally John Armstrong and Gerry Smyth, from my mother, Daphne Siggins, from Arthur Reynolds, and from Roisin Boyd, Cathy Buchanan, Ciana Campbell, Caroline Doherty, Margaret Finlay, Dorothy Fisher, Tony Geraghty, Elizabeth Healy, Cora Lambert, Peadar McElhinney, Joan McGinley, Maeve and Ursula MacPherson, Mary Maher, Fidelma and Fionnan Mullane, Breeda Murphy, Patsey Murphy, Fiachra O Marcaigh, Margaret Stelfox, Maol Muire Tynan, Caroline Walsh – and Dick Walsh, whose enthusiasm was an inspiration throughout.

Photograph credits: Mike Barry: pp.10, 15, 18, 110; John Bourke: pp.54, 58, 59, 60, 67, 74, 75, 86, 87, 91, 110, 118, 174, 179, 182, 183; Tony Burke: back cover (top) and pp.146, 162; Robbie Fenlon: p.111; Leslie Lawrence: pp.46–47, 67, 89, 148; Mick Murphy: p.79; John Murray: pp.2–3, 6–7, 50, 58, 62, 63, 64, 70–71, 78, 79, 87, 90, 94–95, 102, 106, 114–15, 118, 130, 141, 166–67, 170, 178, 180, 182, 183, 186, 187; Frank Nugent: front cover and pp.54, 66, 77, 82, 91, 98, 123, 126, 134, 142, 147, 162, 163, 174, 175, 183; Dawson Stelfox: back cover (bottom) and pp.22, 26, 32, 77, 123, 130, 135, 138–39, 146, 147, 150–51, 152, 154, 158, 163, 175, 190–91. The photographs on p.12 of the 1921 reconnaissance expedition are reproduced by kind permission of Marian Keaney.

✻ *Foreword* ✻

In a divided community, few events attract enthusiasm from all quarters, but for one brief moment in 1993 the first Irish expedition to Everest became a symbol to those looking for an alternative to conflict.

We were there to climb, not to set an example. We revived the tenuous Irish link with Everest by following Howard-Bury's footsteps through Tibet to the North Ridge, scene of the last sighting of Mallory and Irvine in 1924 and still, in 1993, without a British ascent. That mystery, obscure information, and a reputation for fierce technical difficulty at extreme altitude characterised the North Ridge.

A compelling route. A mountain calling.

The media is now preoccupied with individual stardom, and it was perhaps inevitable that much of the public attention has since focused on my reaching the summit alone. This emphasis ignores the commitment and energy of all the expedition members and fails to demonstrate how close we were to getting four climbers on the top, or none at all. There is a fine line between publicly acclaimed success and the ridicule or obscurity of public failure. We have experienced both, and can now recognise their relative values.

Lorna Siggins skilfully avoided such tabloid traps and sent a stream of enthusiastic, balanced, inspiring despatches to *The Irish Times* from the electronic Irish village at Base Camp, attracting a large following throughout Ireland. She was both a detached observer and an integral part of the expedition team. She was astutely aware of the ebb and flow of enthusiasm, commitment, depression that inevitably accompany three months in Tibet, subject to the storms of Everest, the ravages of altitude and the pressures of close expedition life.

Everest may be the ultimate public mountain, but for us it is a temporary target, a moving fixation that, once satisfied, moves on to the next project, the next mountain. Success on Everest, though, has reaffirmed confidence in our abilities, shaken by previous failures, disappointments and tragedies, and has given confidence also to those who know our limitations and thus their own potential.

Ireland has made a minimal contribution to international mountaineering history. But its geographical and cultural position on the edge of Europe has laid down a complex weave of language, tradition and environment – often hidden, never obvious, calling for self-discovery, stamping unique qualities on its people.

We cannot stay silent when brought face to face with the cultural extinction of Tibet and the deforestation of the Himalayas for short-term exploitation. The interest generated throughout Ireland by the success on Everest gave us the platform to express these concerns and led to the formation of the Irish Himalayan Trust. We will support cultural, environmental and educational initiatives for the benefit of the local people of the high mountains. We will support young Irish climbers as they follow in our footsteps, and surpass our modest achievements, returning to a liberal, pluralist society, undivided by prejudice and historical hatred, united by common concerns for the environment and for humanity.

Dawson Stelfox, April, 1994

OPPOSITE:

ON THE NORTH COL (7,000M), WITH CHANGTSE BEHIND. (MB)

✳ *Chapter 1* ✳

'There will be an Irish Everest expedition one of these years. There's bound to be
. . . My feeling is that it should be thinking about the north side rather than the
Nepalese side . . .'

(Joss Lynam, *The Irish Times*, July 1987)

A hot summer night, July 1987, but it was *cold*!

Ice everywhere. The sort of chill that penetrates a groundsheet, a mat, a sleeping bag,
and seeps into hips, neck, shoulders. Finger-numbing, toe-pinching, ear-nipping . . .

Minus 25°C, in fact, and falling again. The climbers had their bivvy-bags, duvets,
they were cocooned in down. My first visit to an Irish mountaineering expedition, and I
was dressed for town . . .

The manager was about to leave for a pint when I arrived, but 'base camp' was easy
to find – a couple of tents, a small scattering of gear, all this among boxes and boxes of
frozen cod and prawns. He had no particular interest in the high outdoors, but he was a
Dublin fish merchant and one of his senior staff had some persuasive climbing friends.
He had agreed to let them spend the night in his fish factory.

The height was hardly adventurous, wind speed was next to nil. As a training ground
for altitude, it wouldn't thicken any blood. But it was a photo opportunity for sponsors
trying to arouse interest in a relatively unknown Himalayan mountain, and the subject
of a few paragraphs for my newspaper, *The Irish Times*, on a quiet Friday night.

Bound for the 7,500-metre peak, Changtse, the climbers were philosophical. When
home's highest point is a fraction of that, what else could they be?

'You've got to know how to walk away from a mountain.' The speaker was cheerful; he
wore his familiar grin. It was a January night in 1988, a packed lecture theatre in Dublin,
six months after I had met Frank Nugent in the cold store. Then, he was looking forward
to a challenge. Now he was looking back on fickle elements and brutal truths.

And failure, perhaps, but with honour – swimming in snow on the slopes of
Changtse as the monsoon closed in early. When Nugent was forced back down within
500 metres of the summit, he was in good company. It was the worst winter on the
Tibetan side of Everest in years. Five other expeditions were stranded at base camp. The
oldest monk in Rongbuk, the world's highest monastery, stretched his memory, but he
could not remember a season like it.

One of the climbers would not forget. He kept a diary of the agony of effort and
weather-bound life in Camp One:

The sun doesn't hit the tent until almost
midday, and when it does it is undercut by a bitter,
thieving wind. The afternoons are icily clear and
the sun shines for a few hours with all the warmth
of surgical steel.

OPPOSITE:
CHOMOLONZO FROM
THE
RECONNAISSANCE
CAMP AT PETHANG
RIMO. (MK) INSET:
THE 1921 EVEREST
RECONNAISSANCE
EXPEDITION.
STANDING, LEFT TO
RIGHT: WOLLASTON,
HOWARD-BURY,
HERON, RAEBURN.
SITTING, LEFT TO
RIGHT: MALLORY,
WHEELER, BULLOCK,
MORSHEAD. (MK)

I wrestled with the boots, stuck zips, gaiters
awry, frozen laces, my fingers too cold to work,
agony gnawing at the bones. The boots were lumps of
ice round my ankles and I was in a frenzy of pain.
Fear too, because I knew my extremities would never
warm up on the long haul up the shadowed moraine
and glacier. I knew I was too far gone – nauseous,
shivering, cursing, keeling over, lying down, crawling
into the tent to collapse on the sleeping bag,
hands locked under me, feet beating the stones outside
with the hollow thud of frozen boots. Over-dramatic,
but I was on the verge of exposure and I had
to fight it.

All night explosive cracks resound deep beneath
Camp One. Winter has arrived, and the glacier knows.
Changtse is a flowing mass of powder and spindrift.
It took a day for the mountain to come into full,
overwhelming perspective. In the afternoon I saw
plumes of powder flowing down the gullies; it
was as if the distant, freezing disaster poured
in through my eyes, down along the nerves to flush out
all the optimism and resolve.

Our route is the size of two alpine faces
stacked one upon the other in foul condition. From
this camp, Changtse, not Everest, dominates the
glacier. Jagged, gullied, corniced, rock-toothed
and rotten-ridged, alive with spindrift and avalanche,
it looms above us with all the malevolence of
a great mistake.

Have we bought the wrong mountain?

More than 50 years before, another Irishman had turned his back on this approach less than a thousand metres below. Lieutenant-Colonel Howard-Bury was no climber, when he offered his services to the Royal Geographical Society as leader of the first reconnaissance expedition to Everest in 1921.[1] Botanist, big game hunter, soldier and spy, he had impressed with his detailed diaries of adventures in central Asia. Most significantly, he was willing to bear his own expenses. He was Anglo-Irish, of Offaly and Westmeath stock. Eton-educated and Sandhurst-moulded, he had cultivated his interest in languages, photography and plants on his extensive travels in India, Tibet and China. His task was to make 'a thorough reconnaissance' of the mountain, the approaches and a possible route to the summit.[2]

LOOKING UP THE
LINGTREN GLACIER
WITH KHUMBUTSE
ON THE RIGHT. IRISH
CLIMBERS, NEAR
CHANGTSE, 1987.
(MB)

Among the climbing team was one man who could not stand Howard-Bury, and the feeling seems to have been mutual. To George Leigh Mallory, a teacher by profession and a young man of liberal views, the leader was 'too much the landlord with not only Tory prejudices, but a very highly developed sense of hate and contempt for other sorts of people than his own'.[3]

It took the expedition one month to get from Darjeeling in northern India to Tingri in Tibet. Food was basic, stomachs were troublesome, and the senior doctor, Alexander Kellas, died of a coronary brought on by dysentery and fatigue *en route*.

The reconnaissance was confused, but successful in exploring and mapping the north side of Everest and identifying a practical route by the 7,000-metre North Col to the summit. It was Howard-Bury's last big adventure; he became interested in politics and humanitarian work. Mallory would return . . .[4]

The lieutenant-colonel's contribution was not forgotten, however. In 1953, when Hillary and Tenzing reached the world's highest summit, he was one of only two people told of the news in advance of the coronation ceremony of Queen Elizabeth II.

There ended the tenuous Irish connection with the region until postcards from Tibet dropped through letterboxes in 1987. The black and white reprint had been borrowed from history to send to Changtse supporters at home.

The Changtse climbers had set out with such promise, such enthusiasm, aware that sceptics within the mountaineering establishment did not share their zeal. The leader, a 63-year-old Dublin engineer and chairman of the Association for Adventure Sports, Joss Lynam, had had a recent coronary bypass – which he viewed at the time as a mere inconvenience.

This was his sixth expedition. Joss was not regarded by the new élite as a technical climber, in the contemporary sense. His strength lay in his organisational ability, coupled with single-minded determination and a surprisingly tolerant nature. Furthermore, he could rise to the occasion. At his very first base camp, in India in the 1940s, he slipped away with a book to learn how to cut steps on ice, hoping no one would notice his inexperience. 'How we survived I don't know,' he observed many years later. 'It was the first real mountain that any of us had ever seen.'[5]

The first major Irish expedition to a Himalayan peak was in 1964. Rakaposhi in Pakistan, at 7,780 metres, was the objective, the route the ambitious West Ridge. Paddy O'Leary was the leader, Joss was second-in-command. There were problems with the porters, who were reluctant to sleep above base camp or to carry above 4,000 metres. An avalanche flattened a camp, injuring a climber. There was friction. The high point was some 6,000 metres.

Rakaposhi was not significant by international standards but it stretched the frontiers at home. There were conclusions drawn: 'On some expeditions, you just get a group of friends together and go,' Joss observed later. 'Rakaposhi was an all-Irish venture, and so it was put together by a non-travelling selection committee. That committee managed to build in two feuds before we had even left Ireland . . . among a mere seven people!'[6]

Compatibility was foremost in Lynam's mind for the 1987 attempt on Changtse. This expedition was scorned by purists. As in other pursuits, but perhaps more so, climbing breeds its own critics.

Balancing organisation with technical skill is the great challenge in planning any expedition. Lynam was conscious that he was seeking people who were not part of the mountaineering establishment. Frank Nugent, Dublin-born and working with the national industrial training authority, then called AnCo, had taken to climbing in his early teens through the Scouts. He was an enthusiast – someone who seemed to get as much of a kick out of paddling a canoe in the Liffey Descent or running a marathon. His genial nature belied his single-minded determination.

In mountaineering, Nugent seemed unambitious, but consistent, visiting the Alps every summer. He did not see himself at the cutting edge of climbing and was unconcerned with the purist attitudes adopted by some of the hard men. One of his most memorable alpine experiences had not been on a summit. It was around 1970, and he was out on the Frendo Spur of the Aiguille de Midi with a friend. The climb involves a long series of rock pitches, leading to a spectacular snow arête. They had reached a high bivouac when a storm came in. Thunder and lightning, and four to five inches of snow. 'Drowned, soaked and demoralised', the pair were forced to retreat. The abseil rope kept getting caught, it was a hard, exhausting day that drew on all their reserves – a day when he learned that mountaineering was not always about success; endurance, 'being there', was paramount.

Frank dropped out of climbing for a while, but he stayed in contact. He and his wife Carol had a family. Their second son, Gavin, had been born with a heart condition. In 1986, they suffered a personal tragedy: Gavin, then aged 11, died.

Joss Lynam approached Frank and Shay Nolan – a Dublin climber who also worked in AnCo – about Changtse some months later. Carol was supportive. Frank threw his energies into fundraising and organisation.

Down in Kerry, a hostel owner, restaurateur and member of the mountain rescue team with a reputation for wandering into fabulous adventures had set a new altitude record for the Republic of Ireland. Mike Barry had made a 6,900-metre solo ascent of Aconcagua in Argentina during the winter of 1984-85. There followed a 9,000-mile river-run with a fellow Kerryman in a small boat down the Amazon, up the Rio Madeira, across the 700-mile Patanal swamp. The boat was smuggled eventually into Bolivia and sold there to a local policeman.

Barry said 'yup' to Lynam's phone call. So did Phill Thomas, a Welshman and a registered mountain guide, who had been climbing for 17 years and had worked as an instructor in the National Adventure Centre in Tiglin, Co. Wicklow. Dermot Somers joined at the last moment. A writer and builder, originally from County Roscommon, he had been a teacher and a diver in a previous life. Never afraid to change direction, he had discovered climbing in his late 20s, and had, in his own words, 'tried to make up for lost time'.

THE TIBETAN PLATEAU HAS THE SENSE OF A HIGH-ALTITUDE DESERT. (MB)

And he did, climbing extensively in Britain and America. His first expedition was with Lynam to the Andes in 1980. But his name was synonymous with Irish 'firsts' on the north faces of the Alps – the Eiger and the Matterhorn. As he observed then:

> Climbing is a means of experiencing clean, steep
> rock or ice, but the Eiger is climbed for the thrill
> of defiant situations, a face to be tackled not for
> the sake of its conditions, but in spite of them.
>
> We watched that north face through pastel days when
> the mountain receded into a smoky-blue remoteness and
> you could slip your thumbnail under the edge and peel
> it off the sky.
>
> Without warning, a storm. A livid glow, as of distant
> cities in flames. Lightning ransacked the ruins,
> thunder trampled the mountain. The Nordwand disappeared
> with a violent sense of extinction.
>
> The true image emerged; squat, ugly, rife with
> geological terrorism.
>
> Oh, there was stonefall all right; and ice-fall, and
> waterfall; and nightfall three times, and when we
> finally escaped onto the neutral summit, we knew we
> had been through a revolution, and that execution is an
> arbitrary vice . . .

In 1980 the Irish invaded Peru. There were two expeditions to the Andes. A Northern Irish group included a young Belfast architect, Dawson Stelfox. The other team, including Lynam and Somers, was from the South, apart from the leader, Calvin Torrans, also a Belfast man.

The Cordillera Blanca of Peru, with peaks of up to 6,700 metres, was the destination for Torrans's group. Then aged 36, his climbing career spanned 15 years, with many alpine seasons and three Himalayan trips. Like Stelfox, he qualified later as a mountain guide.

During the descent from their second 6,000-metre peak, Artesonraju, there was a tragic accident. Tom Hand, a much-loved Dublin climber, disappeared over the north-east face of the mountain. He had fallen about a thousand metres. Despite an extensive search, his body was never found, leaving a devastating sense of loss.

Somers was building a house in Co. Wicklow, designed by his architect friend, Dawson Stelfox, when Lynam approached both of them about Changtse. Stelfox declined, but Somers was keen. He felt he had exhausted his alpine ambitions for the present and was looking for a new direction – the Himalayas. Changtse had already attracted a certain amount of hostile response and counter-response, typical of a small, hierarchical scene. At its worst, it was claustrophobic; at its best, it was funny. Someone within the team had already labelled it 'Snow White and the seven dwarves', inspired by Lynam's white beard and the fact that most of the members were well under six feet tall.

As the highest peak yet attempted by an Irish group, it was no fairytale. It required finance beyond that which the climbers could raise or contribute. Ever pragmatic, Joss enlisted Leslie Lawrence, joint owner of an adventure sports shop in Dublin, The Great Outdoors. A scuba-diver and skier with little or no climbing experience, Lawrence was laid back, relaxed, but had a sharp eye for business. His customers and business contacts were his friends, and he still managed to maintain a professional distance when necessary. Besides, he needed some adventure.

Sponsors need publicity, and so press coverage was arranged through *The Irish Times* in exchange for financial support. Some of the team were uneasy – apart from Rakaposhi two decades before, Irish mountaineering expeditions had tended to shun publicity. There was particular concern about the tendency to give Changtse its alternative title, bestowed by George Leigh Mallory – North Peak of Everest. Was this not likely to mislead? There was no question then, not even a dream, of an attempt on Everest. Or was there – even then – a future plan?

A film crew was enlisted. Danny and Geraldine Osborne, an artist and a doctor living in west Cork with their young children and a South American llama, had won awards for their film work. But the film was never made, the summit never reached. The problems began in Beijing when the Chinese Mountaineering Association increased its peak fee.

Transport problems pushed the group too soon to the 5,000-metre base camp in the Rongbuk valley. One of the climbers, Donal O Murchu, began to show signs of cerebral oedema, a severe form of altitude sickness. He was within hours of death. There was no standby jeep. Frank Nugent and Mike Barry carried him bodily down for miles. It was only after considerable persuasion, when the climbers intended to lie down in front of his wheels, that a Chinese lorry driver agreed to drive him down.

O Murchu recovered in the Tibetan village of Xegar and walked back up to base camp, where there were five other expeditions. The Irish camp was at the bottom of the scale in terms of comfort, while the Japanese (with their six marquees) and the Americans (with solar-heated shower, basket chairs and tables) were at the top. Some dozen Irish and two Chinese, with no Nepalese support staff whatsoever, were squeezed into one family-sized frame tent.

The original plan had been ambitious: to climb alpine style, with no pre-set camps, by the south-west spur, and to descend by the northern flank. It was far *too* ambitious, Lynam acknowledged later.

Frank Nugent had adjusted well to altitude. He slept on the North Col twice. On the second occasion he made a summit bid with Phill Thomas, who had to turn back. Nugent continued until the corniced ridge became far too unstable for further progress. 'I was feeling very strong and if I'd had a companion I might have gone on further. The snow conditions were just too risky,' he said later. 'I wasn't unhappy. But I felt that this was my environment.'

The weather, which had been poor throughout, was to deteriorate further as the expedition prepared to pack up and leave. Death, when it came, was in relatively innocent conditions. Nima, the popular cook on an expedition led by the British climbing legend, Doug Scott, was caught in an avalanche on the Rongbuk glacier only one-and-a-half hours above base camp. Nugent and Shay Nolan helped to dig his body out and strap it on skis. They remarked how light it was and how tranquil and undisturbed Nima appeared to be. He was taken down to the Rongbuk monastery for a cremation ceremony. At this stage, falls of fresh snow had trapped all five expeditions in the Rongbuk valley. The only option was to walk.

It took a gruelling three days. Finally reaching Xegar, the party was told that the main road to Kathmandu was blocked by snow and landslides. They had to drive to the Tibetan capital, Lhasa, where some of the worst riots against Chinese rule since 1959 had taken place. From there, they flew home via Hong Kong. Only Dermot Somers opted for an uncertain, but never uneventful, journey back overland to Kathmandu.

Changtse had been a valuable experience and one which had exposed a persistent flaw in Irish expedition planning – the tendency to set sights too high. 'The route we were aiming for on Changtse was hopeless,' Lynam noted later. 'We should have picked the North Ridge, we should have gone in the spring and we would have got up.'

It had left its mark on all of them, including Nugent, who had tapped hidden reserves of fortitude and stamina at altitude. He had emerged as a potential leader, he had slept on the North Col, and he had seen Everest. For a climber like Somers, it was a particularly painful lesson. He now felt that, up till Changtse, he had been a part of an élite within Irish climbing that had, by its hostile attitudes, induced a type of paralysis.

Fresh attitudes were necessary. At the same time, he sensed the overwhelming nature of altitude and the compromises that would be needed to overcome it. It was the ultimate leveller.

His abiding memory of Changtse was of those last few hours in the Rongbuk valley, when the British expedition had offered to transport the Irish gear out. Dragging their plastic barrels over to the British tents, they had dug deep trenches in the fresh snow. The tracks were clumsy, they were awkward, and they were in marked contrast to those faint impressions left by the skis carrying Nima's body to the monastery. Even in death, their Nepalese friend was in communion with the mountain.

CAMP ONE ON MANASLU. (DS)

❋ *Chapter 2* ❋

Two lonely figures, swaddled in down jackets, one of them weeping his heart out in the Himalayan snow. That's how Frank Nugent remembers the moment on Manaslu, but there was little emotion in the simple diary entry for 27 April 1991:

> 3.30 a.m. Starry and freezing night. Stelfox,
> Nugent, Barry, Somers and Fenlon take full loads
> with a view to an all-out effort to establish
> Camp Three, and beyond.
>
> Good progress to previous high point, then
> deep unstable snow as the slope steepened.
>
> Decision time at the front, the snow was in
> very bad condition, our time was slipping
> away, our porters were already on their way to
> Sama to take us out, prospects for better
> conditions the next day were poor. We resigned
> ourselves to the realities of the situation . . .

This was the Irish pre-Everest expedition to Manaslu – at 8,156 metres, the world's seventh-highest mountain. Three days later, on 30 April, Nugent recorded that he and three fellow climbers began their walk-out by the Larkya La pass, joining up with the Annapurna trail. They had barely reached 6,000 metres. Once again, weather had got the better of an Irish venture. It was such a bitter reminder of Changtse, four years before.

Changtse was never part of one particular climber's map to Everest. Covers fading now, ring-bound expedition reports record his progression and that of fellow northerners like Phil Holmes and Ian Rea. Stelfox, who had studied at Queen's University, Belfast, had been involved in international rock-climbing and mountaineering since 1976. As a boy, he had followed his father, an engineer, out to the Mournes; but he always felt that he had been inspired by his grandfather, distinguished entomologist and conchologist, Arthur Wilson Stelfox. His grandson was invited on his first mountaineering expedition at the age of 19. Bert Slader, former deputy director of the Sports Council for Northern Ireland, had selected seven of the North's most promising young climbers for a trip to the Takht-i-Suleiman (Throne of Solomon) area in the Elburz mountains of northern Iran.

Slader's approach was philanthropic, in combining youth with experience to make up three teams of hard climbers, mountaineers and trekkers. The 21-strong group included Rory McKee, who was to accompany a film crew on the 1993 expedition to Everest. That 1977 trip had its own film team from the BBC. Among the crew of five was a fresh-faced reporter, then based in the BBC office in Belfast, named Jeremy Paxman.

Now presenter of BBC television's *Newsnight*, Paxman recalls that the expedition had two objectives – to climb in the Elburz but also to explore the Valley of Assassins, named after the Ismaili sect which was notorious in the 12th and 13th centuries for stabbing its religious and political opponents, mainly Muslims and some Crusaders, while under the influence of hashish. For him, it was a break from the relentless cycle of shootings and killings in Belfast, but he would have enjoyed it more if he hadn't been affected by altitude. As for a young architectural student by the name of Stelfox, of him he has no recollection . . .

When Stelfox arrived in the Andes three years later as one of five students on the Northern Ireland expedition, the same system prevailed. They travelled widely among the mountains and many peaks were climbed. Dogged energy, good humour and great interest in what was going on were some of the characteristics that struck Dermot Somers when he first encountered Stelfox and his fellow students at Fair Head, Co. Antrim, and in the Mournes. They were tightly knit, these Queen's University climbers – generation after generation bonded by a common interest. Some of them were not particularly proficient, but this did not matter to Stelfox who was both loyal and generous in the support that he gave his friends.

It was a time when club structures were more evident in climbing, but Stelfox, nevertheless, needed external challenge. He pursued it in the company of climbers like Ian Rea and Dermot Somers. The contact was mutually opportune. Not many of Somers' contemporaries were willing, or financially able, to disappear off to the Alps for six weeks to two months; not many people had good cars. Stelfox could, Stelfox had.

Like Somers, his interests extended beyond climbing. In marathon debates, Stelfox could be forthright and argumentative, eager to pursue logic, while Somers might be keener on cultural and philosophical dimensions. If there were differences, they were those of intellectual temperament; they were both ambitious, but shared an infectious sense of fun.

They climbed together, at times spending long periods in the Alps on meagre resources. Both had to work hard to achieve what they wanted, and Somers was always relieved when his friend appeared suitably exhausted. Stelfox betrayed no sense of success as something that came naturally, even if at times it did.

He was, however, very well able to organise. It was a quality which attracted some and repelled others who feared commitment or resented managerial ability or suspected that there was something slightly indulgent about it all. Like Somers, Stelfox did his classic north faces in Europe including the Grandes Jorasses, the Matterhorn and the Eiger, and climbed extensively in Ireland and Britain. He had no interest, though, in the sunny havens of the New Rock Climber – California and the south of France, where technical performance reigned and adventure was less important. He still hasn't climbed in either area, although Somers revelled in both locations.

His first of some ten Himalayan adventures was to Bhagirathi in 1981 with Ian Rea and Tommy Maguire. Bubbling with enthusiasm, Maguire had taken up climbing when he was in the British Army and had continued when he left. They made the first ascent of the North face of Bhagirathi II in the Garhwal in northern India. It was an enjoyable climb of considerable quality, entirely on snow and ice. On the descent, there was a fatal accident. Tommy Maguire fell. By the time help arrived, it was too late.

The pain surfaced in a piece Stelfox wrote three years later, on his return from another Himalayan peak, Churen Himal. He described life below a solitary rock outcrop just below 6,000 metres:

> The weak warmth of the afternoon sun fades to the
> chill of a clear sky and an icy wind. We scurry into
> the sleeping bags, anxious to hibernate before the
> coming winter. There is no such thing as relaxation
> on this climb: it is too big to enjoy.
>
>   Every minute is part of the battle to keep control
> over the environment; relax and you sink into the
> insidious downhill slide of dampness, dehydration
> and depression . . .
>
>   My mind wanders back almost three years to when, in
> the same tent, I lay between Tommy and Ian on our
> fourth night on Bhagirathi. We were jubilant with
> success but muted by exhaustion. Inexperience ignored
> the dangers of dehydration and we drank little.
>
>   The next day was Tommy's last and the overwhelming
> frustration at the futility of our efforts of aid
> is still with me. The body only runs on empty so
> far . . .[1]

Tommy's death – a year after Tom Hand had gone missing in the Andes – was a devastating event and one that was to have its effect on the future relationship of his two companions. Their achievement on Bhagirathi was the most significant new route in the Himalayas by Irish climbers at the time. Yet it was completely overshadowed; they could not forget.

There was another deep wound within 12 months. Angela Taylor was a young medical student at Queen's who took to climbing with enthusiasm and flair. She was popular, and was particularly close to Dawson. Late that season, the Irish were in the Alps. Stelfox was with Ian Rea on the Walker Spur, while Angela Taylor was with another group on the Peigne. Somers was on the north face of the Dru. The Walker Spur pair were caught in appalling weather conditions and there was some doubt as to whether they would survive. They did, and made it to the top, in the most extraordinary display of Irish alpinism to date.

Exhausted, exhilarated, Stelfox arrived back in Chamonix to a tragedy. There had been a freak accident on the Peigne, when a less experienced French climber had fallen, pulling down rubble. Angela Taylor was knocked to her death.

The next few days were a nightmare of dealing in broken French with undertakers and police, making the arrangements for the return of her body, with Somers trying to support Stelfox as best he could. Yet for years afterwards, he felt that there was a darkness in his friend – a core of private suffering – and a compulsion to burn immense amounts of energy.

Dawson Stelfox and Calvin Torrans pursued careers in mountain guiding, a qualification based on years of intense training and commitment. Dawson's dedication to architecture did not flag. His life accommodated both careers. He thought nothing of setting off to Scotland for a weekend of hard driving and winter climbing. Responsibility was offered him in everything he tried, and he rose to it. The Matterhorn marked a coming-of-age: he grew into the role of leader then.

Barely a season passed without trips abroad, some more notable than others – Stelfox to the Karakoram in Pakistan in 1986, and Torrans on a British expedition to Makalu, one of the five great Himalayan 8,000-metre peaks, in 1989. The Irish Shimshal expedition, as the Pakistan trip was billed,[2] had started out as a less than serious trip; the instigators were Paula Turley, a doctor and by then one of the outstanding women climbers, and Margaret Magennis, who had taken up climbing while studying law at Queen's and who was to marry Stelfox a few years later.

Makalu, by contrast, was a serious undertaking by big names in British mountaineering. Torrans was the only Irishman. The aim was not only to make the first British ascent of the Tibetan 'great black one', but also to attempt a traverse. That winter, *Irish Mountain Log* recorded that Makalu I had had to be abandoned because of heavy snow which had exposed the slopes to avalanche.[3] Two members of the team had climbed a new route on the west face of Makalu II, also known as Kangchungtse, and some time had been spent on other 6,000 to 7,000-metre peaks. It was no secret that there had been a split, and that the venture had been marked by individualism and discordance.

With the same breath, in the same paragraph, the log noted that 'the Irish expedition to Manaslu in 1991 was officially launched at a press conference in Clondalkin Leisure Centre on 26 November, with Chris Bonington as a distinguished guest'; and that Dawson and Margaret Stelfox, with Dermot Somers and Maeve MacPherson – orienteer, climber, administrator at the National Adventure Centre in Tiglin and married to Somers – were currently climbing in the Chulu Himal in Nepal. They hoped to make a reconaissance for Manaslu.

Manaslu, 'mountain of soul'; it was to leave a taste, one that was sour rather than insipid. Picture four faces smiling out of the autumn 1990 issue of *Irish Mountain Log*: Calvin Torrans, Sir Edmund Hillary, Harry O'Brien and Frank Nugent. The Everest summiteer had made acquaintance with a 'previously unknown substance', turf, on a short tour of Wicklow; he had talked of his Irish grandmother, who had inspired him as a child with

OPPOSITE:

APOCALYPSE ON MANASLU, 1991. (DS)

her stories of sailing from Ireland to New Zealand and up north through the Pacific to work as a governess. On his visit, Hillary had also agreed to be patron of the Irish 1991 Manaslu expedition.

It all started happily enough. Three years earlier, Nugent had returned from Changtse, disappointed but charged with enthusiasm for big mountains. He had slept on the North Col; he wanted to go back. He joined forces with Dawson Stelfox and a two-tier or twin-peak approach to Everest was conceived. It would begin with Manaslu and it would attempt Everest in 1993. Himalayan names had become a throwaway currency on the Irish climbing scene.

Stelfox had already provisionally booked the fierce West Ridge of Everest in the name of the Mountaineering Council of Ireland, but Nugent preferred the North Ridge. It was more realistic, in the light of the Changtse experience.

But Manaslu was first. In December 1989 a letter arrived at his home in Belfast from the Nepali agent, Bikram Neupane. The Ministry of Tourism (Mountaineering Section) of 'His Majesty's Government of Nepal' had granted the Irish group permission for the peak in the spring season of 1991.

A loose panel had already been formed, meetings had been held. Aims had been identified: to tackle an 8,000-metre peak; to gain some experience and credibility; to use it as a springboard for Everest.

The route on Manaslu would be by the north-west face, the normal approach. It would require a substantial team of some 140 porters for the walk in to base camp. The climbing panel would reflect a North-South dimension, and would be led jointly by Dawson Stelfox and Frank Nugent, with Mike Barry, Martin Daly, Robbie Fenlon, Phil Holmes, Gary Murray, Harry O'Brien, Donie O'Sullivan, Dermot Somers and Calvin Torrans. Leslie Lawrence and Nick Stevenson would act as joint base camp managers, and a film crew of John Murray and Bill Forde, both of RTE television, would make a one-hour documentary.

'Twin Peaks' read the headline in *The Sunday Tribune* of 10 March 1991, the first in a series of expedition reports. The scene was set with brief biographical sketches: Stelfox, a mountain guide and freelance architect; Torrans, a mountain guide, also from Belfast, now living in Co. Wicklow; Phil Holmes, a mountaineering instructor from Kilkeel, Co. Down; Gary Murray, an outdoor education instructor, also from Northern Ireland.

There was Nugent, a training manager with FÁS, the industrial training authority; Harry O'Brien, also with FÁS. Somers was described as a builder and writer in Co. Wicklow; Martin Daly, a garda (policeman) living in Dublin; Mike Barry, a restaurant-owner from Kerry; Robbie Fenlon, an outdoor education instructor; and Donie O'Sullivan, a doctor from Dublin.

Stelfox and Nugent had been keen to include some younger climbers who would benefit from the experience. 'To climb with the likes of Frank Nugent, Dermot Somers and Dawson Stelfox is the equivalent of a young aspiring cyclist to ride (*sic*) in a team with Stephen Roche or Sean Kelly', the report gushed.

Fenlon and Somers were climbing partners. As the youngest, Robbie had a lot to catch up on. A motor mechanic-turned-climbing instructor, he had spent many Sundays as a boy with his parents on hill walks in Wicklow and Connemara, before borrowing a rope and heading off with his brother to Dalkey quarry in 1984. He had followed the usual progression – rock-climbing in Dalkey, Glendalough, Fair Head. Then came Scotland in winter, routes in the Alps with Somers, and it was on his fourth season that he climbed the Walker Spur with Clare Sheridan. They had climbed the spur over two days until rock gave way to a snow trough, a blue Italian sky and 'a beautiful, breathless summit'. It was a place and time that would affect him for the rest of his life: 'Nothing to show for it, of course – but the confidence to keep on trying. There are distant peaks in the future, uncertain journeys waiting in the wings . . .'

Donie O'Sullivan was on Manaslu to 'rest his elbows', since he had developed tendonitis the year before. Good-natured and mildly sardonic, he was one of Ireland's finest young rock-climbers, with an impressive international record, as Somers observed:

> The kind of rock-climbing Donie, Robbie and the young
> climbers do has long passed the limits of normal
> human possibility and entered the realms of physical
> transcendence, a kind of levitation, fingertips
> smeared on blank verticality, launching the body
> across simian overhangs. It's no longer a question
> of neck and natural talent; modern rock-climbing demands
> intensely trained stamina, and like any other
> Olympic-standard athlete, Donie knows he has a
> limited time at the peak of the sport. In a way,
> a Himalayan expedition is a sacrifice of golden
> time for him. Still, if it rests his elbows . . .
>   'But mountaineering lasts a lifetime, and he and
> Robbie have chosen to bring both sides of their
> sport with them, to go for the broad experience.

So if young climbers were chosen for the experience on Manaslu, where were the women? At least three had been considered, according to Stelfox. At that time, the three most experienced were considered to be Paula Turley, Moira Rea and Clare Sheridan, the latter a teacher with a fine climbing reputation, married to Calvin Torrans and the mother of small children. Clare and Calvin had always taken the view that if one was climbing, the other should stay with the family. The couple had agreed that Calvin should go to Manaslu. It may not have been apparent at the time, but it was a decision that was to govern two expeditions.

Paula Turley offered an ideal combination of skills, as a fine alpine climber with Himalayan experience and a qualified doctor. She, too, had young children and was not

MANASLU (8,163M). PICNIC AT CAMP TWO WITH (LEFT TO RIGHT) DERMOT SOMERS, ROBBIE FENLON, MIKE
BARRY, FRANK NUGENT, DAWSON STELFOX, AND (BOTTOM RIGHT) HIGH-TECH FOOD BOX. (FN COLLECTION)

available. Moira Rea, married to Ian, declined; it was said that she felt that she did not have enough experience.

Should the women have forced the issue ? In hindsight, perhaps yes. If there were no women on Manaslu, how could there be any on Everest? A great deal of 'serious' time was spent debating it at the planning stage, but the climbers say that it was never resolved.

There was even a reverse fear of tokenism among the climbers, and a recognition that one female in an all-male team could be 'difficult'. The expedition was already large, it was argued, and if two were invited the numbers would pose a problem. Already irritations and tensions were developing among the male members who had been invited for a variety of reasons – experience and competence being the priorities at the expense of compatibility.

It was a rush. British Airways had agreed to sponsor the flights to Nepal, but there was a misunderstanding over the publicity agreement. The climbers did not receive the tickets until a day before departure, after some of them had agreed to abseil down the front of the Shelbourne Hotel in Dublin for photographers. Frank Nugent, who tended to burn both ends of the candle at the best of times, was in a state of shock and exhaustion by the time he arrived in Kathmandu. Stelfox, Somers and Fenlon had flown out a week before to link up with the expedition agent, Bikram Neupane; to clear freight through customs; to complete the formalities and to shop for fresh supplies. Somers was to write a series of reports for *The Sunday Tribune*:

> We stacked four tons of food and gear in the hotel
> conference room and broke it down into scrupulous 28 kg
> loads. Then the bulk of the expedition crashed
> raucously into the modern/medieval dazzle and dust
> of Kathmandu, strung out on jet lag, tension and
> free in-flight drink, courtesy of British Airways,
> which flew us out and will doubtless fly us back
> thinner, lighter, strung out on altitude and elation.[4]

✸ *Chapter 3* ✸

No one had taken them that seriously. Was it just wild talk? Ama Dablam is a most popular Himalayan peak in the Khumbu area of Nepal. There had been eight ascents in 1990 alone; an Irishman, Brendan Murphy, was a member of a successful British expedition. But it is a 'difficult and challenging target', as the *Irish Mountain Log* noted when reporting plans by a party of six men from Munster to tackle the 6,800-metre mountain by the South-west Ridge.

Public interest, such as it was, lay in the pre-Everest expedition to Manaslu. I had just returned from trying to make sense of the outbreak of civil war in Yugoslavia for *The Irish Times* when I got a phone call from Joss Lynam. He wanted to report a new altitude record for Irish climbing. A Co. Cork climber, Mick Murphy, had sustained frostbite on a solo ascent of Ama Dablam.

The expedition had been led by a mountaineer and tour guide from the Gap of Dunloe in Co. Kerry and co-ordinator of the county mountain rescue team, Con Moriarty. 'After the initial scepticism, and taking into account Mick's ability and strong, self-reliant, nature, the best (and only!) course of action for us was one of total support,' he wrote afterwards.[1]

Moriarty and fellow Kerryman, Mike O'Shea, had originally been selected to lead the climb, alpine-style. However, an outdated tin of pineapple had put paid to that. Both developed acute food-poisoning, and O'Shea ended up in hospital while Moriarty tried to recover as best he could at base camp.

'After he crossed the bergschrund onto the upper face, we knew his commitment was definite and his "wander" was for the summit,' Moriarty continued in his account of Murphy's progress. 'Watching through binoculars and telescope from the four base camps in the valley below, everybody grew nervous. He was like a lone "fly" on a huge tapestry – steadily moving up.'

At 5.30 p.m. on 4 April 1991, Moriarty saw Murphy reach the summit 'amidst the last rays of the sun which had followed him up the west face'. He spent about 30 minutes there, photographing the Tricolour flag of the Irish Republic which he had carried with him, absorbing the view. It was two days later when he hobbled slowly and painfully back into base camp with a severely frostbitten right foot.

Murphy's bid came as some surprise to those who did not know him. A graduate of building construction from Thomond College in Limerick, Murphy had learned his first trade – and developed an interest in outdoor education – in the army initially. On leaving college, he had taken up instruction in canoeing, sailing and mountaineering, recognising it as a commercial opportunity. He had a reputation for fearlessness, if not technical skill. He would, in the words of one climber, 'slap, punch, chop, kick his way up a mountain with tremendous energy, almost leaving his teeth marks on the rock'. It was his first expedition to Nepal.

You walk for hours through paper-bark birches, or on dense pine-needles between tall trunks, the exposed roots polished by countless feet. Then, out through a spray

OPPOSITE:

CREVASSE AND SERAC: RANRAPALKA, CORDILLERA BLANCA, PERU 1980. (DS)

of white butterfles, a scatter of rhododendron blossom, onto a cliff-face and a safe, stupendous path along a cunning terrace that overhangs a river far below.

At the time, Dermot Somers was reporting back to *The Sunday Tribune* in Dublin from the Manaslu expedition in another part of Nepal:

People will always travel, climbers will always climb. It is the manner that counts. Thinking of the attitude with which we might attempt Manaslu without greed or arrogance, I am reminded of a scene from the third day of our walk-in. By the icy waters of the Buri Gandaki, a Nepalese fisherboy with a bambo rod and a hand-held reel perched serenely on a boulder, casting, casting. The turbulent flow gleamed silver in late sunlight. He showed us every trick he knew, including the way to smile when nothing is more important than a smile.

At last his line tightened, the rod bent, a length of silver water lifted flicking and flashing out of the river onto the bank. We could have had it, for we were friends. I saw how a fish is the spirit of water, and the summit the spirit of a mountain, and how certain fishermen, who are never hunters, catch the river.

In contrast to their compatriots on Ama Dablam, the Irish Manaslu expedition never did reach the summit. There were hints of trouble early on.

'In the mountains, weather becomes a state of mind,' Somers wrote:

Windless sunshine is euphoria. Starlit frost at night and you sleep easy, firm conditions in the morning. But snowfall is paranoia. It banks up in the mind, like fear at night. Will it snow for days on end, storming the mountain, smothering it in a treacherous shroud, wiping out the way to Camp Two, drifting over these tiny tents, roaring down slopes in deadly avalanche? . . .

In the middle of the night, someone heroic shuffles around, shovelling snow off our tents. It becomes easier to breathe. Towards morning, the snow ceases; not dramatically, more an acknowledgment of its own tedium. Saving itself for later? The night is alive with powder-avalanches pouring off steep faces. Camp One is safe, but paranoia nags . . .

In the morning, the mountains clash against a
harsh, clear sky, their jagged ridges almost audible
in the cut-glass air. For a few minutes Camp One
hangs suspended between night and rational day, in
a crystal bowl of ice, snow and shadow. The sun
scrapes up over the saw-toothed peaks of Ganesh,
dawn floods the frozen scene and the icy stillness
thaws.

Dawson Stelfox, up to his shins in snow, is on the
radio, a 6 a.m. call to base camp. We're going
down, but never mind! Yesterday we pushed through to
Camp Two at 5,600 metres by the dramatic Naike Col.
We looked over the other side of Manaslu at new
mountains and austere Tibet, dumped gas and equipment,
and beat a tactical retreat to Camp One.

Several climbers had already approached 'personal bests' well before Camp One.

They had all reached the summit of Europe by long,
arduous routes on the sustained rock and ice of Mont
Blanc, and here they were, on mighty Manaslu, plodding
ironically up steep juniper slopes patched with snow,
feeling like Sisyphus and his boulder of gravity,
without any of the glory or myth. I remembered the
first time I passed this height, in the Andes, pulling
up on cactus stumps rooted in loose gravel!

At this point, on Manaslu, there comes a naked,
overwhelming awareness that the entire height of the
Alps, *from sea level to summit*, still rears overhead,
while the thin air grows thinner by the metre. And yet,
it doesn't actually *look* like that. The ice-fields
slope away towards an attainably foreshortened summit,
and we point out the obvious line with extravagant
gesture – past the Naike Col, dodging steep seracs to
the North Col, then up a chilling apron of ice, and
onto the long, long summit ridge . . .

Sherpas were among those who had died on the slopes of Manaslu – ten alone in 1972.
The Irish group felt morally responsible for their Sherpa team, and were opposed to
offering bonuses in return for greater risks, though there was a divided opinion on this:

Dendi, our talented and versatile Sherpa-cook, has
more high-altitude experience than our entire
expedition put together. He has
climbed several major peaks, and it is his ambition
to climb Everest. We might argue among ourselves
whether this is for the sport, or the money. On our
expedition he remains firmly at base camp, well-paid,
and up to his elbows in porridge and curried potatoes.
      No one would dare tell Dendi to go easy on the spice;
his satirical black eyes and whiplash grin look back
at you with affably superior intelligence.
      'Sir –' he answers.
      'Don't call me sir! *Please*, Dendi . . . '
      'Okay, sir . . .'[2]

Ten days after they had established Camp One, over six feet of snow fell. They were stuck
in it at 16,000 feet – 'trapped on a snow platform somewhere above a rumbling shunting,
goodsyard-and-ghost-trains-glacier'.

Persistently, we dig the tents out, and now they
huddle in little bowls well below the level of the
snow. These mountain tents are small, that's how they
save weight, and though the materials are space-age,
breathable, super-wrap, you're still buried in a
tight little tomb with the relentless, indifferent,
couldn't-care-less snow banking up against it; at
first it presses in the sides like a tightening rib-
cage, you whack the fabric and the dark shadow slides
back, only to pile deeper, wider, denser. Gradually
it lies against the domed curve of the roof, blocks
the phantom light, and weighs down on the lungs.
      In the middle of the night I hear the laughter of
the snow – the airy, inhuman whisper of a cosmic
joke; work and plan for two years, fly halfway
round the planet . . . to hurtle head first into the
seventh highest snowdrift in the world where the
map said Manaslu. You can see the joke yourself . . .[3]

On 12 May 1991, *The Sunday Tribune* reported that 11 Irish mountaineers had
abandoned their attempt on Manaslu owing to weather conditions.[4] 'As it was, six of the
11 had already given up,' the report read. 'Five – co-leaders Dawson Stelfox and Frank

Nugent, Dermot Somers, Mike Barry and Robbie Fenlon – made it to 21,000 feet, about 5,000 feet short of the summit.'

'We took a mountaineer's decision,' the report quoted one of the group as saying, 'and turned around.'

In a separate report Somers wrote:

> There are very few footprints on the world's highest
> peaks this season. Last year, on one record-breaking day alone,
> 35 people stood in turn on top of Mount Everest. So far,
> towards the end of this pre-monsoon climbing season,
> no one at all has reached that summit. Manaslu too,
> only 3,000 feet lower than Everest, remains untrodden
> despite the attentions of four major expeditions –
> Irish, Ukrainian, Italian and Swiss.

The snow had always been too soft, too deep – too much, Somers wrote, with a hint of despair:

> On those mornings, we sat out at Camp Two, watching
> thick clouds boil up in the Nepalese valleys to the
> south, swelling and subsiding, but sure to engulf us
> in the afternoon – while an opposing army of gloomy
> cloud moved in from the lower mountains of Tibet, and
> the two fronts collided over Manaslu. Towards the end,
> these frustrating conditions split the expedition
> predictably; five climbers clung to acclimatisation
> at 18,500 feet (Camp Two), while another group of
> six orbited base camp and the lower slopes.[5]

Frank Nugent's comment afterwards in *Irish Mountain Log* was tight-lipped: 'Sure! We had some tensions about tactics and style, should we have been on the hill at all, in the conditions that developed.'[6]

The same issue noted that half the expeditions to the Himalayas had been unsuccessful that season, and that two members of a South Tyrol expedition to Manaslu, led by the very experienced Hans Kammerlander, had died while descending from an unsuccessful summit bid. One had been killed by a fall on easy ground, the other by lightning. One of the Irish team quipped morbidly. 'If it had happened to us, the murder-squad would have been called in.'

If there was a certain economy with the truth, it was in the interests of diplomacy. The visiting Manaslu support trek was unaware of the tension. Yet as the grains of silver gradually form a dark-room print, so a picture began to emerge from stories told in the months that followed. Stories of personal initials on food bags and gas cylinders; stories of gear evicted from tents, of supplies divided to the exclusion of the support team. Stories of disagreement on tactics, on style. Far below the summit of Manaslu a team affair had split in two.

The mountain was dangerous; the mountain wasn't technical; the route was old-fashioned; the method was madness; the selection was flawed; the film was a liability; the costs were too high. This was one climber's impressions of a row in the expedition's dying days, as five of them descended, having abandoned Camp Two. The essence of the dispute was the nature of an expedition – whether referred to with a big or small 'e', Dermot Somers wrote:

> In the early days of big mountain climbing, the
> emphasis was on heavyweight, national teams which
> dug in at the foot of a climb like the base of a
> pyramid, and then piled climbers and camps on top
> of each other till the tip of the pyramid coincided
> with the mountain top.

This was the 'siege' approach, which depended on collective nouns like organisation, leadership, tactics, co-operation; and on money, for it was expensive too. Himalayan climbing had gone lightweight, daring in style, he continued:

> Climbers train seriously, acclimatise scientifically,
> and make light, fast summit bids working solo
> or in self-sufficient pairs, rather than as a team.
> Individual achievement has become a priority, and
> the new style has thrown up super heroes like every
> other sport. Of course these systems have always
> overlapped in practice, but the Irish Manaslu
> expedition has opted a little awkwardly for the
> small 'e'.[7]

Such pressures had revealed the fault line in Irish mountaineering, with Dawson Stelfox and Calvin Torrans on opposing sides. Both from Belfast, they were separated by philosophy and by factions which developed around them. It was a division that had made it difficult to form expeditions. Frank Nugent felt that this could be overcome by ignoring it or appealing to a common interest which he believed would resolve all differences of style and personality. Stelfox was not so optimistic, but felt that climbers like Torrans and Ian Rea were necessary for the 8,000-metre attempts ahead.

Yet the hostility was deep-rooted, complex and palpable from early on in preparatory meetings. If there was one positive aspect to the whole affair, it was that it steeled the collective nerve for an attempt on Everest which would be based on compatibility and co-operation above all else.

No one could deny the quality of Stelfox's leadership under trying circumstances – 'endlessly inventive, motivating, energetic and diplomatic,' Somers wrote. The style was democratic, but persistent. He led by example, setting a pace that drew others along in its wake. He had been born with 'iron filings in his blood, perpetual motion in his soul'.

There was an example of this on arrival at Camp One. As the rest of the group flaked out on the backs of rucksacks, Stelfox began probing the area with a telescopic rod, picking a slope and beginning to dig a snow hole. The others joined in, Somers recalled, digging two entrances about 12 feet apart which met in the centre. 'After three hours of exhausting labour at 16,000 feet, Mike Barry – no mean miner – shook his head behind Dawson's shovelling back. "This is a bit bloody Irish," Barry quipped. "He's going to tunnel his way to the summit!" '

And there was a lesson. A lesson that one of the most important skills in mountaineering was the ability to deal with failure, to transform it into a 'triumph of the spirit'. It required an attitude that was anathema to the militaristic assault, battery, conquest.

> You never *conquer* a mountain; mountains are
> indomitable and can absorb you like a snowflake . . .
> Instead, you conquer your own weaknesses and fears,
> you come to terms with luck and the weather, you
> build yourself into the strongest, most durable
> snowflake you can be, and with enough willpower
> you *may* reach that summit where the real world
> comes to a final, breathless point and you can
> go down into life again, fulfilled.

It seemed no coincidence that both Stelfox and Nugent were ill for some time after the Manaslu expedition. Stelfox developed hepatitis, and it would be a year before he felt really fit again. It was a year after, also, that Joss Lynam wrote Manaslu's epitaph. I was up at his house, looking for a reference from his extensive library, when the subject came up in conversation. He pulled out a book from his laden shelves – an account by the Austrian, Karl Herrligkoffer, of the ascent of Nanga Parbat in 1953. Flicking through the pages, he grinned as he found what he was looking for:

'Of nine members of the team, six have remained my friends.'

The members were different. The sentiment remains the same.

The agreement had always been that the Everest team would be picked following Manaslu. It had become obvious that there would have to be radical changes. Irrespective of that final arbiter, the weather, a technically experienced team was no longer sufficient.

The new team was announced quietly. Then, as Stelfox recalled, 'all hell broke loose'. But events have their own momentum, and a telex arrived from China.

> We agree in principle fr yr expdn to come to
> climb Mt Everest fr pre-monsoon 1993. Fr details
> yu may contact our TMA* later tist regive tlx
> to TMA* since they have no right to book out
> mountaineering expdns.

* Tibet Mountaineering Association

❋ *Chapter 4* ❋

There were two ways of leaving Manaslu in April 1991: the Buri Gandaki route, which was the quickest and which the porters were taking, and the alternative by the Larkya La, the 5,105-metre (16,700-foot) pass lying between the Buri Gandaki and Marsyandi valleys which was part of the Annapurna circuit. Nugent, Barry and Fenlon had chosen the latter. Torrans, O'Brien and Murray opted for the former, accompanied by Stelfox, who felt he should stay with the porters.

Somers would have gladly opted for the Larkya La, but was anxious to offer Stelfox as much moral support as he could. They were withdrawn, keeping their distance from the main group. There was little conversation.

He had recorded the descent in his diary. The return from Camp Two was a 'surprisingly sensual experience'.

> We had been up above the snowline for almost a
> week and when I emerged onto the dark-green slopes
> below, the warm savoury scent of juniper was mildly
> intoxicating. Brilliant clumps of tiny, blue flowers
> had sprung up between the bushes, and the eye
> and heart lavished an almost excessive
> affection on them. You realise at once how bleak,
> colourless, odourless it is above the snowline,
> although it has its own stark brilliance of light
> and line . . .
>   I realised in an unsettling way how easy it would be – almost a
> relief – to turn one's back on the cold, harsh
> mountain with a shrug, and return to warm, green,
> real life. However motivation, purpose, challenge
> are ingrained, you leave part of yourself and your
> imagination on the mountain, and you have to return
> and reclaim them; a resolution is necessary –
> whether it is success or failure is not the most
> important point, but you cannot simply walk away
> on a whim. The shadow of the mountain will
> follow you a long way.

Was it the mention of a name? On the walk-out, one hot, dusty day of unrelenting terrain, picking their steps along a dried-up river, Somers tried to banish the shadows. He and Stelfox began to talk of Everest in an anxious, desultory fashion. In the hostile after-light of Manaslu, there was little room for optimism. Somers suggested Richard Dean . . .

Both of them knew the six-foot-eight psychotherapist very well. Married and living as Richard O'Neill-Dean in New Zealand, he was an accomplished climber who had worked for a time as senior instructor in the National Adventure Centre in Tiglin, Co. Wicklow. Dawson had climbed and worked with him also.

He was, unmistakably, of Anglo-Irish stock. The family farm lay near Navan in Co. Meath – rich, rolling countryside with barely a hill, let alone a crag, in sight. Richard had taken up climbing as a pupil at Portora Royal School in Enniskillen, Co. Fermanagh, the Alma Mater of Samuel Beckett and Oscar Wilde.

The attitude of the headmaster at the time, Percy Rogers, was liberal. He was supported by school rules which delineated the boundaries as 'the lake and its shores' (the school is beside the magnificent northern border lake, Erne) and 'the ocean and its shores'. The headmaster's father, Bruce Rogers, was a mountaineer.

Among Richard's regular climbing partners were schoolfriends Anthony Latham, who was to pursue a career in medicine, and Richard Shackleton, a direct descendant of Sir Ernest Shackleton, the Antarctic explorer of Irish Quaker stock. Perhaps such influences explain what it was about Dean that evoked another era, combining a 19th-century explorer's determined, ascetic air with a most engaging sense of humour. One could imagine that he might have turned to the sea, if he had not been drawn instead to mountains. Although he was technically proficient, he felt that he lacked courage and drive.

Winter climbing in Scotland and seasons in the Alps led to a memorable ascent of the Walker Spur with Anthony Latham, an early Irish achievement performed entirely on 19 Mars Bars. With a degree in agriculture, he went to South America where he worked as a research assistant on the British Colombian Amazonas Expedition studying rain forest agricultural systems.

Richard Shackleton flew out and the pair climbed in Colombia, Ecuador, Chile and Argentina in 1979 – the Leinster Andean Expedition! O'Neill-Dean returned to work as a manager of a 150-acre sheep farm in Laragh. His rock-climbing began to develop again, and he put up several routes which have continued to give him a sense of pleasure, marked by moves which hinge on a long reach.[1]

He was drawn to outdoor education, and to instruction work in the National Adventure Centre in Tiglin, then run by Paddy O'Leary. It seemed to offer an attractive alternative to mucky fields with hungry sheep and to the 'mud and misery' of farming in an Irish climate.

Through his work in adventure sports, particularly with disadvantaged groups, he became interested in psychoanalysis and eventually trained and qualified as a psychotherapist. He worked as a counsellor and therapist in addiction treatment, before opting to emigrate to New Zealand with his partner, Frida O'Neill, and a young family.

O'Neill-Dean had a strong sense of Irishness, which may have become more significant to him in New Zealand. He was aware of the build-up, and of Manaslu, but was too engaged in his career and family in Dunedin to get involved.

He was delighted to get the phone call. Would he come to Everest? Of course he would, making a conscious decision to tell Frida that this was what he wanted to do. 'I felt it was a mistake of Dawson and Dermot to think of me,' he said afterwards with typical self-effacement. 'In their state of dehydration, emaciation, exhaustion and part-hallucination, leaving Manaslu, perhaps they recalled in some distant past my name. Perhaps they felt that even a bovine presence like mine was better than what they had.'

He came over a year before departure, spending time with Stelfox, Nugent and Somers and meeting Robbie Fenlon. He first encountered Fenlon in Dalkey quarry when he thought he caught him tearing off bits of bush and heather and generally 'desecrating' one of his own routes. He was impressed with the general sense of purpose and the professional approach to the expedition. He recalled discussing it with Frida, and noting then that there was one person among the group who would either climb the mountain or not come back alive. He was to be proved right, later on.

There had been few meetings after Manaslu; relations were tense, and there was a continuing dispute over funds and gear – whether any surplus should go towards the Everest expedition or to individual members. By September 1992, there was a tacit decision that five from Manaslu would certainly form the backbone of the Everest project – Stelfox and Nugent as leaders, with Barry, Somers, Fenlon. O'Neill-Dean would make six. And a second emigrant would be the seventh.

Tony Burke was living and working in Cardiff as a computer officer with the University of Wales medical school. The young, hard, Dalkey quarry *aficionado* had taken up climbing when he was 13. Fresh-faced, eager, confident, courageous, he hung out with whoever would have him. He was among the first to use chalk in the quarry, and to wear resin-based rubber climbing boots, hitch-hiking from Dublin to Belfast and back to get them in one day. Competition to put up new routes was keen: Burke, the 'guru', left his chalk marks and earned his place in the Dalkey climbing guide.[2]

On finishing school, he took a degree in applied physics. He went to Scotland, to the Alps, to North America, bristling with gear and good humour. He left his chubbiness behind, and became a lean, strong, technically proficient rock-climber with a reputation for persistence. He had adopted an attitude early on which he attributed to the influence of his father, a Dublin hypnotherapist named Tony Sadar, to 'live every day as if there is only six months left'.

On one alpine trip, Burke was descending the Flammes de Pierre and was about to traverse onto the base of the famous Bonatti Pillar on the Dru when he and his partner saw three Japanese climbers in trouble. They had taken the wrong route off the Dru and had been caught in an horrific couloir. A rock hit the top climber, the second one was also pulled off, and both fell to their deaths. The one uninjured climber wore big and clumsy boots, had no English and was in a very distressed state.

Boots or no boots, Tony took the distraught survivor back up the mountain, over the summit in a blizzard, and down the long descent to the hut. The thoughts of the Japanese climber on finding himself summarily bereaved and climbing the Dru for the second time went unrecorded.

Tony had been invited to join the team for Manaslu, but he pulled out when his wife, Joanne, a paediatric nurse, became pregnant. 'A climber can be selfish, but you can't be too selfish,' he had remarked afterwards. His turn was to come again.

After Ama Dablam, still elated, Mick Murphy delivered a boat to the Canaries from Cork and was due to fly home briefly and then on to Pakistan. On the morning he was due to leave Gran Canaria he went out angling and hooked a thousand-pound marlin. He was reeling it in for four hours, wondering if he should abandon it and catch his plane.

He hung on, missed the flight and caught the fish. Complications left him with just a few hours in Cork before heading east. It was only when he was sitting in Flashman's Hotel in Rawalpindi that he was able to catch his breath and open his post. There was a letter from Dawson Stelfox; it was a formal invitation to Everest.

The team then was Stelfox, Nugent, Somers, Barry and Fenlon – all of whom had been on Manaslu – with Murphy, Burke and O'Neill-Dean. Stelfox was still keen on further Northern participation among the climbers but it was not to be. Ian Rea and Gary Murray were both invited, but they declined.

The Manaslu base camp management of Leslie Lawrence and Nick Stevenson had worked well together. Supported by his business partner, Gerry Collins, Lawrence responded positively. Both he and Nick Stevenson of the Surf Mountain equipment shop in Belfast would be invaluable in raising sponsorship.

Stevenson had known Stelfox since schooldays, at the Royal Belfast Academical Institution (RBAI). Both had taken up climbing and had continued at university, where Nick studied electrical engineering. Climbing was, in Stevenson's view, 'always something I had to work at'. He spent time in the Alps and was on the 1980 expedition to the Peruvian Andes with Stelfox. He opened his adventure sports business, Surf Mountain, in 1984 with a partner, Chris Thompson.

Flying to Nepal was the worst part of the Manaslu expedition for him. Two years before, he and Thompson were returning from Heathrow to Aldergrove airport in Belfast when a British Midland Boeing 737 crashed onto the M1 motorway at Kegworth and split in two. Forty-four people were killed and over eighty were injured. Thompson was badly hurt and was lucky not to lose his legs. Stevenson was conscious after the impact and managed to scramble out of the side of the aircraft.

When the opportunity arose to return to the Himalayas again with the Everest expedition, he volunteered for the first seven weeks. He couldn't ask more of his business partner, and this was the period when he would be most useful.

So where were the women, or was this just an aspiration? The fact that no women had gone to Manaslu now appeared to pose a problem. Inclusion at this stage could smack of tokenism, if those with enough experience were not available. There was debate, but no decision; inevitably, the result was bad feeling, guilt and misunderstanding, traces of which were evident for some time after.

If there could not be a woman climber, the key positions of doctor and technical assistant to the film crew offered possibilities. After Manaslu, Donie O'Sullivan had felt that Everest was not for him. He had not acclimatised well. Geraldine Osborne, doctor on Changtse, was approached, as was Paula Turley, again. Neither was available, both being working mothers with young children.

Dr Stephen Potts, a 40-something paediatric surgeon working in the Royal Belfast Hospital for Sick Children, was recommended as a keen mountaineer. Also a poet and ornithologist, Potts had been on Mount Kilimanjaro and was due to travel as doctor with an expedition to Aconcagua in Argentina in early 1993.

Potts was interested, as was Dr Kathy Fleming. In her early 30s, she had come to medicine late, having first studied pharmacology, and was by then a partner in a general practice in Hillsborough, Co. Down. She took a year off after medical studies to back-pack her way around North America, across to the Pacific islands, to New Zealand, Australia, south-east Asia, Hong Kong, Nepal and India. She had done some hill-walking and basic climbing while at university in Edinburgh, but tennis and hockey were her sports.

A third name was under consideration, someone who had spent time as a volunteer in Nepal, mainly on veterinary work. There was a period of mistaken identity; when Stelfox met Kathy Fleming, he spent hours dissuading her . . . under the impression that he was speaking to a hardened Third World veteran with particular expertise in castrating dogs.

Because of work commitments, it was agreed that Potts and Fleming should split the estimated three-month expedition between them. Stephen would cover the first six weeks, and Kathy would travel out for the second half. As a further boost to the Northern Ireland representation, Stelfox asked Rory McKee, with whom he had been to Nepal the year before, to accompany the film crew.

McKee, an outdoor pursuits instructor from Comber, Co. Down, had climbed Mount McKinley in Alaska, Mount Cooke in New Zealand and various peaks in Nepal. He had also climbed in the Arctic, principally on the island of Spitsbergen, and had travelled to the Antarctic with the British survey of 1983.

Dawson and Margaret Stelfox, Rory McKee and a couple of other climbers went on a climbing trip to Nepal and Tibet in the spring of 1993 to confirm arrangements with the expedition's trekking agent, Bikram Neupane. They spent four weeks around the south side of Everest, climbed Lobuje and Island peak, and then flew with Bikram to Lhasa to agree a budget with the Tibet Mountaineering Association.

By then, the expedition had co-opted John Bourke on to the organising team. A senior executive with one of the country's top financial institutions, Allied Irish Banks, he had taken early retirement to pursue a variety of interests. Still in his mid-50s, Bourke's passion was rugby, but he was also a keen athlete, a sailor and a hill-walker. After four years in the US during the post-Kennedy era of the 1960s and two years in Holland, he

AKA RAJ, ASHA RAI, MIKE BARRY
JOHN BOURKE, TONY BURKE, DENDI SHERPA
DHAN BAHADUR RAI, DOARJEE SHERPA, ROBBIE
FENLON
DR KATHY FLEMING, BRIAN HAYES, JANGBU
SHERPA
KHUNKE SHERPA, GAO LANG ZI, LA WANG

LESLIE LAWRENCE, RORY McKEE, MICK MURPHY
JOHN MURRAY, FRANK NUGENT, RICHARD
O'NEILL-DEAN
DR STEPHEN POTTS, DERMOT SOMERS, DAWSON
STELFOX
NICK STEVENSON, LORNA SIGGINS
(ALL PHOTOS, LL)

had returned to Dublin where he joined Allied Irish Investment Bank. By the end of the 1980s he was managing director of the bank's investment division, representing it on a number of company boards, and had excellent business contacts. He had also spent his first of three 'informal' seasons with climbing friends in the Alps.

He met Frank Nugent, then bound for Manaslu, at a dinner in honour of Sir Edmund Hillary in 1990. Bourke inquired about money; the situation was not promising. What was the budget?

'Forty thousand,' Nugent had replied, tentatively.

'So I'll give you one per cent,' Bourke had rejoined cheerfully, then persuading two of his dinner companions to do likewise. Within minutes, Nugent had three cheques in his pocket. 'Only 97 per cent now,' Bourke had said, smiling.

A few months after Manaslu, Chris Bonington was in Ireland to give a lecture on a trip to Greenland – the hard way, of course. Bonington had an affinity for Ireland; the Sugarloaf in Co. Wicklow had been his first mountain. John Bourke went to hear him and met Dermot Somers. He inquired with enthusiasm about plans for Everest. A mental note was made.

Bourke had his own plans. He had taken early retirement. The financial lure meant little to him now, if it ever had. He and his wife Moya were active, their family was growing up. His first project was an Atlantic sailing trip to the West Indies, and he was barely back on dry land when he got a phone call. A meeting between Bourke, Nugent and Somers was arranged.

The banker did not need much persuading. Yes, he said, he would act as treasurer and financial adviser for the Everest expedition. His real task would be to raise the money that he had agreed to manage. Nugent estimated it as £110,000. Bourke thought for a little, did a few sums: it was more likely to be £150,000.

The climbers were cautiously elated. Here was someone who could offer them not just contacts, but corporate credibility. It was a dimension they had never aspired to before.

Oxygen became an issue in the mountains of Mourne, during a training weekend to coincide with Richard O'Neill-Dean's visit from New Zealand. He arrived jet-lagged, but elated. Most of the team was there. They did a little climbing and a lot of talking over two long days.

Originally, the plan was to climb Everest unsupported: no oxygen, no Sherpas. It was a purist approach and reflected the thinking of the leader, Dawson Stelfox. Many of the established Irish climbers would have squared their shoulders with a steely glint in the eye, and agreed.

And Somers? Perhaps five years before, but not now. He was convinced that it was unrealistic. Reaching the North Col during the Changtse expedition of 1987 had been a formative experience. If that was how 7,000 metres felt, he had no illusions about the amount of air 1,848 metres higher still. If he had any residual doubt, it was to be dispelled by subsequent experience of Himalayan altitude.

He argued at length against unrealistic aspirations. This was the first Irish attempt and success on Everest was a slim enough prospect. On their chosen route, it was slimmer. None of them had any experience whatsover of real altitude, he said.

The summit was far closer to 9,000 metres than 8,000. The main difficulties on the North Ridge were concentrated on a long traverse above 8,000 metres. This would have to be reversed in descent, an enormous duration at that extreme altitude. Research into previous climbs on the north side had indicated that only a handful of individuals had succeeded without oxygen so far.[3]

Stelfox was still unconvinced. One of the reasons for choosing the northern route had been to reduce, if not to eliminate, the need to hire Nepalese as support staff and expose them to risk. In the 40 years since Hillary and Tenzing Norgay had stood on the summit of Sagarmatha – the Nepalese word for Everest – the skilled Sherpas of the Solo Khumbu had paid a heavy price on the southern routes for their ability to withstand high altitude.

Richard O'Neill-Dean was unequivocal in his support for Somers's position, while Nugent, the diplomat, also gave his tacit approval. O'Neill-Dean would not consider going above 8,000 metres without oxygen, although he would willingly carry loads for anyone wishing to do so.

The debate continued, broken only by sorties to the crags and a cheerful message by phone from Tony Burke. He was enthusiastic; he had no doubts. Yes, he was going. It was an uncomplicated, unconditional, response that was to give a fresh charge to the whole venture.

A brochure was produced to outline the approach. Food and equipment would be transported by yak to Advance Base Camp below the North Col, at 6,500 metres. Beyond this point, it said, the climbing team would be 'self-sufficient, carrying all food and equipment without Sherpa support'.

All eight climbers had summit ambitions, it said, and success would be determined by 'weather, health and acclimatisation'.

Chapter 5

John Bourke knew that he had his work cut out for him. He would be pursuing a small pool of sponsors likely to be interested in supporting the Irish Everest expedition. Undaunted, he set up meetings, he wrote to friends. Dublin and Wicklow-based members of the expedition found themselves talking to senior executives in some of the country's top boardrooms. In each case, the formula was the same – to display the Manaslu photographs, state the current position and present them with a copy of the Manaslu film, *Summit of Soul*, made by Murray Media. Somers found himself at many of the meetings, shoulder to shoulder with executives on first-name terms with Bourke. It posed difficulties, as he recalled:

> Problems with my wardrobe – no jacket!
> Paul, a young climbing-friend insisted I take
> his for a crucial meeting. It was a trendy
> little item, disco-crumpled, one button.
> 'I can't wear that, Paul! This is a
> serious meeting. We're looking for a
> Hundred Thousand Pounds!!'
> His jaw dropped. 'A Hundred Thousand Pounds!?
> You don't need a jacket, Dermot; you need
> a balaclava and a shotgun.'

Sir Edmund Hillary's agreement to become the expedition patron was important, but few sponsors would know of his Irish grandmother. Further endorsement was required. With this in mind, Bourke wrote to the President, Mrs Mary Robinson, seeking her support. Anne Lane, her secretary since 1969, was a keen hill-walker who had been away on a trek to Everest base camp in Nepal in November 1990. The President's personal adviser, Bride Rosney, replied warmly with an offer of a reception whenever the team departed. It was a significant leg-up for the expedition's credibility.

By December 1992, when he produced the progress report in the form of a newsletter with Frank Nugent, Bourke was feeling confident. The report named the team, the sponsors, the professional advisers, the subscribers to an Everest 200 club, details of support treks, and outlined the planned media coverage. The original aim had been to raise 50 per cent of the funds in Northern Ireland and 50 per cent in the Republic. By mid-November 1992 some £130,000 of the targeted £150,000 was within sight. 'Although we are in good shape, we are not there yet,' Bourke wrote.

It had been a difficult and exhausting process. The 'quick money' tended to come from the individual contributors. Indeed, Bourke's Everest 200 club read like a 'who's who' of Irish business, or at least those representives whose suited arms he had been able to twist. The first corporate sponsor was secured through Nick Stevenson. One of his customers in Surf Mountain was Sam Torrans, chief executive of the Northern Bank.

Early on, the Government's sports council, Cospoir, which had set a precedent by giving a grant of £5,000 to the Manaslu expedition, indicated that it was prepared to offer £20,000 for Everest. Con Haugh, its senior executive, was very enthusiastic; he had taken a personal interest for some years in the activities of the Mountaineering Council of Ireland. It took some negotiating, when Bourke had to draw in his political contacts, to get the cheque. The Northern Ireland counterpart offered £5,000.

The minister responsible for Cospoir had pointed out the educational dimension. This potential for the involvement of schools captured attention in an unexpected quarter. A friend of Bourke's who was manager for Colgate toothpaste in both Britain and Ireland, introduced Bourke to Ted Hession, managing director of Colgate-Palmolive Ireland Ltd. At a lunch attended by Bourke and Lawrence, a deal for £30,000 was struck. Colgate would be the major sponsor; Advance Base Camp would be named after it. The pressure was off now, but there had been much disappointment, dismay and dogged persistence. The climbers were used to rebuff, and most did not expect instant sponsorship. Sometimes they had to reassure John Bourke. They recognised it as a business deal: nothing for nothing.

The Scout Association of Ireland expressed support – a welcome gesture, given its extensive network. Lowe Alpine, the gear manufacturers with an Irish base in Tullamore, Co. Offaly, agreed to give some £16,000 worth of equipment. Aer Lingus Cargo, a subsidiary of the national airline, offered to fly it all out and to give a subsidy towards tickets. There was other assistance in kind: after some negotiation, the army offered the use of two mess tents for Base and Advance Base Camp. A select few sponsors were demanding.

Bourke was asked the same question over and over again: what media coverage would there be and how would it be transmitted? Well, by satellite, he replied, and promptly began to chase this up. The state telephone network, Telecom Eireann, gave £10,000. However, the 'satpack' – that crucial piece of equipment which the expedition peddled for months – was leased by ABB Nera and Ericsson's.

Friends of climbers and friends of friends of climbers bought up the t-shirts and the postcards which would be posted back from the mountain. An Everest party hosted by Tom and Jane Fenlon, parents of climber Robbie Fenlon, raised £1,000. A club was formed to run the support treks, which were to be led by Damien Cashin and Tom Clear of the Call of the Wild trekking company in Co. Wicklow. After a couple of slide shows, places on the three treks of 30 days' duration were quickly booked up, at £2,900 per person. This would raise another £10,000 for the expedition.

The negotiations for media coverage reflected the expedition's professional approach. *The Irish Times* newspaper, which had supported Changtse, responded favourably through its news editor, John Armstrong. The newspaper promised sponsorship of £5,000 and coverage, as did 98 FM, Dublin's most successful local radio station, which had access to a regional audience through its highly successful independent radio news network.

The state broadcasting service, RTE, was prepared to give coverage only, but had already agreed to provide materials, equipment and editing facilities to the Murray Media film crew. It would screen the finished film in both English and Irish. If it was feasible, some footage would be sent back to use in news broadcasts. After some persuasion, the broadcasting company agreed to part with £2,000 in cash.

Meetings were set up to confirm the details of the coverage, which now also included Downtown Radio in Belfast. Soundings were made with Pat Kenny, host of a mid-morning radio show and weekly television programme on RTE. Kenny, an engineer by training, was interested in this kind of thing. *The Irish Times*, which had adopted it as a suitable theme for its schools supplement, wanted exclusive print media coverage as a condition of its sponsorship.

How to juggle these demands? It was to exact all the diplomatic skills of the experienced John Bourke.

Nobody told me. As a newspaper reporter, I knew that writing the obituaries would have to be one of my first tasks. 'Profiles', I called them, when I interviewed the team.

It was shortly before Christmas 1992, with just three months to the expedition's departure date, when *The Irish Times* features editor, Gerry Smyth, had phoned me at home. I had, he recalled, written about the Changtse expedition in 1987 when still a freelance journalist. As a sponsor, the newspaper had been invited to send a reporter on one of the expedition treks – given the bureaucracy associated with Tibet, this was the most pragmatic approach. He was a little taken aback at the positive response.

Though it might suit the expedition, the first trek made little sense from a daily newspaper's point of view. Two tall, fleece-clad climbers came in to the editor's office to discuss these points. It was agreed that I should go on the third trek which would arrive at Base Camp around about the time of the estimated summit bid.

Next time we met, it was in a draughty warehouse on a dark January afternoon in Dublin's dockland, during one of two weekends devoted to packing some four tonnes of freight in blue plastic barrels. The expedition had 'borrowed' space in the warehouse from the Dublin branch of a pharmaceutical multinational.

Eat! Eat! Eat! Drink! Drink! Drink! Such was the advice from Mary Moloney, nutritionist at the Dublin Institute of Technology in Kevin Street College in her detailed assessment of the climbers' nutritional needs at higher altitudes. The daily energy requirement would be 5,000 to 6,000 calories climbing and 3,000 to 3,500 resting, she had estimated. Dehydration would be the greatest limiting factor: when climbing, she had advised, drink five litres of fluid a day.

Her menu would be used as a trolley-filling guide during a stint of free shopping in Musgraves wholesalers in Dublin, a faithful sponsor of past adventures. Standing over a scales in the warehouse that Saturday afternoon, one climber was making up muesli, one was stripping unnecessary packaging, and one was measuring sachets of isotonic drink. Somers had assumed the role of temporary camp quartermaster, noting numbers, contents and colour-coding of barrels for the manifest.

(TOP) ÁRAS AN
UACHTARÁIN.
PRESIDENT MARY
ROBINSON
AUDITIONS FOR A
PLACE ON THE TEAM.
(JB)
(BOTTOM) DAWSON
STELFOX TALKS TO
THE IRISH MEDIA VIA
SATELLITE-
TELEPHONE,
PROMPTED BY LESLIE
LAWRENCE. (FN)

The detailed 11-page list recorded everything from snow anchors to Spam to bags of herbal tea, with the equipment for the film crew of John Murray and Brian Hayes taking up an uncommon amount of weight. There was a general air of subdued activity as volunteers, including some of the first trekkers to pay deposits for their trip, came, did their bit and went.

With Dr Stephen Potts now on Aconcagua, Kathy Fleming had taken full responsibility for a substantial medical kit, much of which had been supplied through sponsorship. She was under particular pressure, as she had become engaged to be married. The wedding would take place in Belfast, the honeymoon in Spain, just a couple of weeks before she was due to leave.

Interviewing each of the climbers in the chilly warehouse kitchen for the 'profiles' and a preliminary article for *The Irish Times*, it was interesting to record their observations. Stelfox, Nugent and Somers talked in great detail about the choice of route. There had been little need for persuasion when Nugent came back from Changtse, full of enthusiasm for a return to the North Col.

Since Everest had been climbed, only a handful of expeditions had chosen the North Col to North-east Ridge route, or North Ridge route for short. Since their disappearance in the mist in 1924, it had been synonymous with the two British climbers, Irvine and Mallory. The dearth of interest in this approach was largely due to the difficulties of gaining access to Tibet which had been closed to foreigners after the Chinese occupation in 1951.

There was also the challenge posed by the route itself. Few in the west had believed China when, having realised the political capital that could be made of mountaineering achievement, it had claimed the first successful ascent of the North Ridge in 1960.

There were no photographs; two Chinese and one Tibetan had arrived up on the summit in the dark, it was reported. There were similar western doubts about a second Chinese North Ridge expedition in 1975 which, like the previous one, had relied heavily on Tibetan support. Two Chinese and seven Tibetans had made it; one of the Tibetans, named Phantog, was the second woman to climb Everest – a mere ten days after the Japanese mountaineer, Junko Tabei, on the South Col route.

The doubts about both efforts were to be dispelled in time; in the case of the 1975 team, there was independent confirmation of its success later that year when British climbers Doug Scott and Dougal Haston found an aluminium survey tripod on the summit after their ascent of the South-west face.

Tibet was opened up to foreigners again, unofficially in the late 1970s and officially in 1984. Mountaineers were among the first parties to be given permission. As the English climbing writer, Audrey Salkeld, has noted in her book, *People in High Places*, climbers were 'easy enough to contain and single-minded enough not to ask too many questions' and the peak fees were a useful source of hard currency.

There had only been a handful of successful expeditions on this route since then. Japanese climber Yasuo Kato, who made three Everest ascents in a decade before disappearing on a descent in 1982, chose the North Ridge route on his second success in 1980. He was followed by three members of a Spanish Catalan expedition in 1985, four Japanese, one Chinese and one Nepalese on the heavy-duty Asian Friendship expedition of 1988, and 21 American, Russian, Ukrainian, Kazakh and Tibetan members of the 1990 International 'peace' climb.

None of the expeditions had tackled North Ridge ascents without oxygen, although there were some individual records in May 1990. The route had exacted a heavy toll. The deaths of Mallory and Irvine, who had last been sighted 'going strong for the top' somewhere above 8,300 metres, were the most celebrated. On that same expedition, in 1924, a Nepalese and an Indian, Shamsherpun and Manbahadur, had also died – of a brain haemorrhage and of pneumonia following frostbite, respectively. Two years previously, on the second British Everest expedition, seven Sherpa staff were lost in an avalanche below the North Col.

Despite a revolution in mountaineering equipment, the death rate was still running at about 1 in 30. The climbers played down the risk and the low average rate of achievement. On this route, success was estimated at about 36 per cent. Instead, they stressed the positive aspects. The other side of the mountain had become completely devalued. There were 32 pairs of bootprints on the summit from the South Col route on one day the previous year. Some 268 foreign and Nepalese climbers had bumped shoulders down at base camp, and tensions had run high.

Elizabeth Hawley, Reuters' Himalayan correspondent based in Kathmandu, had recorded the atmosphere in the Nepalese English newspaper, *The Independent*.[1] Spaniards and Dutchmen threw stones at each other, she wrote. A bitter row broke out between American, New Zealand and Russian expedition leaders about the use of the route. The British complained to the Nepalese ministry of tourism about a Czech who, according to the British leader, had been 'wandering all over the mountain'. There were claims that the Russians were helping themselves to other expeditions' food and tents. She quoted a despairing Sir Edmund Hillary: 'What's happening to this sense of remoteness and adventure?'

'If one just wanted to get an Irish team to the top, the South Col via Nepal is the obvious choice,' Stelfox told me then in his January 'warehouse' interview, referring to the 'heavy duty, loadsamoney' approach which saw the summit as the only goal. The North Ridge route was more difficult, more interesting than the South Col, but with fewer 'objective dangers' such as the unpredictable Khumbu ice-fall which had been claiming an average of two to three lives every year, mainly Nepalese.

It would not involve a large Sherpa team, he stressed. Most significantly, the three Changtse veterans knew this route as far as Camp One on the 7,000-metre North Col. The ascent would not be all 'fingertip stuff', but would involve two technically difficult stages – from Advance Base at 6,400 metres to the 7,000-metre North Col and over the last 400 metres to the summit. The arduous, immeasurable and unpredictable effects of altitude would always be the main encumbrance.

Stelfox flinched at the term 'leader' and at any mention of military terms like 'conquest' and 'assault'. He preferred to describe himself as a co-ordinator: 'It's not as if I am taking a group of Scouts. I am not making decisions on people's behalf.'

The altitude, and the higher stakes set by Everest, would impose great strain on the individuals, he agreed. 'Just because we know each other now doesn't mean we won't have rows. I'm fairly rational and can accept people behaving irrationally. I've seen it many times before.'

Nugent conveyed confidence, secure in the knowledge that much of the preparation had been done and that there was a policy document.

'When I think of the rush to get off for Manaslu . . . I was boggle-eyed then by the time I got to Kathmandu,' he told me in the warehouse kitchen. He had adjusted well to altitude before, and was familiar with the route to the North Col. As for oxygen, it would be 'the ultimate in optimism to think that we could afford to leave it behind'.

The weather would be the one variable. The pre-monsoon season did offer more stable conditions. Still, Joss Lynam had always described Himalayan weather as being 'about as predictable as an Irish summer'.

As the afternoon drew on, Dermot Somers took his turn in the kitchen 'confessional', describing in detail the difficulties of living at altitude with less than 50 per cent of normal oxygen levels. 'It always sounds like a very hostile environment but it is absolutely the best place to be. One pays a certain price in physical exertion and tolerance for being in the last true wilderness. If it were just a slog, people would not want to go back. We always want to go back. It's the aesthetic quality of being in the most magnificent places, surrounded by like-minded people with a tremendous commitment that counts.'

Mountains were well able to split one's mind – a recurring theme in his fiction writing. 'Half of you says that the summit is the essential goal, half is happy to be there and to accept what happens.' He had never been a competitive mountaineer, he said; he had started too late. It was experience that counted in the Himalayas, the experience of recognising one's limits and knowing when to stop.

The question of women was raised. A couple of leading women climbers had been approached, but were unable to accept, both Stelfox and Somers explained. For women with children, three months away in such an uncertain environment was too much of a sacrifice. Somers also expressed regret at the fact that there were not more younger climbers. It was at this level of Irish climbing that there was so much dynamic activity, he stressed.

It was obvious that they regretted their inability to bring everyone with them, but there was no hint of defensiveness here. A quota system would not work on an expedition. It would be hard enough to get a high altitude effort to work with a small group of hand-picked men . . .

They invaded Scotland for the last bit of training and a photo-call with a Colgate photographer on Aonach Mor. They did routes on Ben Nevis, and returned exhausted

(TOP) *IRISH TIMES* LITERARY CRITIC, EILEEN
BATTERSBY, ANALYSES FOOD BARRELS IN A
DUBLIN WAREHOUSE WITH DERMOT SOMERS.
(JB)
(BOTTOM) DR KATHY FLEMING DIVIDES THE
MEDICAL SUPPLIES. (JM)

LUNCHTIME
CONCERT. (JB)

but exhilarated. This was compounded, Stelfox noted, by a marathon drive home through the night to get Robbie Fenlon and Tony Burke back in time for an appearance on a morning television show. Already, the business deal was making its demands.

Then it was down to the dockside warehouse again for 'another shift on the packing line'. The army tents were the last to be labelled. Five hours before the air-freight deadline, the last nine barrels were filled.

LEAVING DUBLIN ON ST PATRICK'S DAY. FLIGHTS, AND SPRIGS OF SHAMROCK, COURTESY OF AER LINGUS.

(JB)

❃ *Chapter 6* ❃

It was on everybody's lips: someone wondered if the airport might be closed. As Aer Lingus staff in Dublin talked quietly of their own nightmare early yesterday morning, three passengers bearing boots and ice-picks slipped quietly away to chase a few dreams . . .

(*The Irish Times*, 11 March 1993)

Television lights. Cameras. Microphones. Crowds and cheers. Perhaps it should have been like this, but Dublin Airport was still dusting itself off, shaking and waking itself up when three rucksacks on trolleys were wheeled into the departure area on the morning of 10 March 1993. There was to have been a breakfast reception, but no one quite knew where.

The press officer for Aer Lingus, the national airline, looked as if she hadn't slept a wink. It had little to do with these Himalayan-bound passengers: an advance party of Dawson Stelfox, Dermot Somers and Nick Stevenson, base camp manager, were leaving for Nepal. Her mind was on far more serious matters – the airline was in serious financial difficulty and her phone hadn't stopped ringing the night before.

The main party was not due to leave for another seven days, on St Patrick's Day, but two of the main sponsors had decided that they wanted to get their publicity moving now. Almost four tonnes of equipment had been flown the 4,844 miles from Dublin to Kathmandu in a record 14 hours, reporters were told. It sounded mighty, but it was a modest load compared to some international mountaineering efforts. The 1975 Bonington-led ascent of the South-west face had commanded 24 tonnes of equipment from Britain – delivered overland!

Frank Nugent, Joss Lynam and Richard O'Neill-Dean had come to see the first three off. As they waited to be called through their gate, they seemed calm, confident. Much of the packing had been done weeks before. I was out there chatting and casting the odd envious glance at their day-packs. Would mine be as compact in a month's time? I remembered that I had some work to do. A quote for *The Irish Times*, Mr Stelfox?

He swung around, eyes dancing. 'Excited!' he whispered. And disappeared.

Arms no longer feeling like pincushions after so many medical shots, the full expedition had had its first gathering two days before. As she had promised, the President, Mrs Robinson, had received climbers, support team and spouses at her residence in the Phoenix Park. It was a formal occasion. She valued the group's North-South dimension, she said, and referred to some 'in house' expertise – her secretary and Himalayan trekker, Anne Lane. She was 'curiously aware' of the contribution of past Irish climbers like John Tyndall, the President continued – Tyndall being the renowned scientist from Co. Carlow who had made the first ascent of the Weisshorn. Her parting words: 'May I wish you a safe and fulfilling climb.'

O'Neill-Dean towered above everybody else at the President's reception. He had been in Ireland for about ten days with his wife Frida and two little girls. 'A representative

VILLAGE LIFE, NEPAL. (JM)

for Irish emigrants in their millions,' he had told me when we met for the first time in Bewley's café in Grafton Street for a chat, But he was under no illusions, he added quietly, before Frida arrived. 'There can't be anything much more dangerous than the top 400 metres of Everest, certainly on this route, so the idea that everybody on this team is going to get to the top is unrealistic.'

Once more, he had stated his position. 'I see myself as contributing to the base and middle of that pyramid – making sure that someone gets to the top.'

Becoming a parent had changed his perspective on high-altitude mountaineering, he said. It had reinforced his belief in the three basic aims – to come back, to come back friends, to come back having climbed the mountain. How had he felt when he had got the first phone call asking him to come? He gave a wry smile. 'It was more like being drafted. You couldn't refuse.'

These sentiments were echoed in a hurried press release which Frank Nugent had put together for the airport farewell. It bore all the hallmarks of midnight oil. 'We promise only honest endeavour in our quest to reach the summit of the world and wish Dawson and his advance party a safe journey at the start of this great Irish adventure,' it had bubbled.

A week later, on 17 March, a dozen singing trekkers bade goodspeed to the rest of the group, as Aer Lingus hostesses showered them with shamrocks. This was St Patrick's Day.

HOLY MAN, WITH TRIDENT, KATHMANDU. (JM)

The party had little time to regroup in Kathmandu. Stelfox, Somers and Stevenson had made all the preliminary arrangements with Bikram Neupane, the shopping for spuds and other fresh food was done, the freight had arrived, more or less. Within a couple of days, they were on a cramped Nepalese bus, bound for their acclimatisation trek in the Helambu-Langtang area north of Kathmandu.

Bed-tea in the mornings, chapatis and porridge, striped umbrellas for the sun. Such was the experience for the expedition and for three groups of trekkers supporting the expedition who followed the climbers' bootsteps in the Langtang over the next few weeks. In each case, the bus would leave the city on a Monday morning for the hour's drive to Sundarijal, a little village north-east of the capital at about a thousand metres. Six days later, it would return, this time to Dhunche, 112 kilometres from the city, to pick up some weary, some footsore, some sick bodies, all in a state of exhilaration.

Accompanied by a Bikram team of Sherpas, porters, kitchen boys and a sirdar – most of whom came from the Solu Khumbu region of Nepal – the groups took the Langtang route through the tiny mountain villages of Kutumsang, Mangegot, Ghopte and Gosainkund where children with strong Tibetan features called for chocolate and sang their greeting, 'Namaste'.

Terraces and stone cottages were left behind as the trail snaked through lush forests of rhododendron, shading primula and gentian and juniper bush and cobwebs of lichen. As the air grew thin, conversations would falter – boot upon rock and the tap of a ski pole the only regular sound. The beautiful but barren Himalayan landscape emerged above the cloud and snowline at 4,500 metres.

The weather had been particularly bad for the climbers, and they had been forced to dig their way through the Laurebinayak pass into Gosainkund. Eating in mud, sleeping in tent puddles had been bad enough further below, but their discomfort seemed nothing compared to that of the Nepalese porters who wore flip-flops or fragile canvas shoes and tied their heavy loads together with light string. The trees became stunted, frostbitten shrubs, terracing disappeared as they moved higher and higher towards the pass, grappling with altitude and struggling through snowdrifts, descending at last towards Gosainkund's frozen lake.

The ice was a carpet, covering the infamous black rock which is said to be the head of Lord Shiva. The god created this lake – by accident. He took some poison, and prodded a glacier with his trident to quench his raging thirst. The waters are said to run by a 60-kilometre subterranean channel into the Kumbeshwar pool in Patan . . .

Whatever the truth of it, Gosainkund became a centre of pilgrimage and still attracts hundreds of lunar tourists during a full moon festival in August each year. Slight headaches could be left behind here, for the trek was on the descent . . . down past yet another 'Everst Hotle' offering views of Mapuche and Annapurna and down to sub-tropical forest again. Lemon tea at 3,200 metres was at Sin Gompa, a sacred Buddhist temple under slow but steady restoration, with its own yak cheese factory nearby.

Rhododendron was virulent, the forests were ripe with silver birch and larchpole pine. They slid in more mud and rain down into Dhunche, where houses seemed to topple into yards, and yards ran into narrow streets. After so many days of silence, broken by birdsong, they were struck by the level of activity in the Trisuli river town – people cooking, cutting, chatting, mending, laughing, living with animals and children at their feet. A couple of hostels had limited electricity. The chemist had divided his shop: one section for locals, one section for tourists seeking 'upset stomach pills'.

The tents pitched, the meal cooked, they waited for their transport here. The bus would take them on the rough and rutted track back to beds and showers and bookshops – and a brief recovery – in Kathmandu.

Hens, dogs, pigs, half-clad children. Women hunched with hammers over rocks, breaking them down into gravel. Men building bridges by hand over the Sun Khosi river. There are at least 13 checkpoints on the rough road from Kathmandu to the Friendship Bridge on the Nepalese-Tibetan border.

Tibet. Little mention had been made of the Chinese colony in the flood of publicity before the expedition left Ireland, beyond reference to some 2,500 US dollars in peak fees which had been paid over to the Tibet Mountaineering Association in Lhasa. Another 60,000 US dollars would be paid over for trucks, yaks, yak herders, liaison officer, interpreter.

Then, mountaineers make perfect tourists. They won't ask awkward questions: they

OPPOSITE:

TRADITIONAL NEPALI
PORTERS, MALE AND
FEMALE, CARRY
LOADS SLUNG FROM
THE FOREHEAD BY A
HEADBAND. (JM)

just want their climb. Or will they? Dermot Somers had been there once before, as had Nugent, Lawrence and Barry. Somers knew what he was returning to when he saw the red Chinese flag flying over the busy border trading post of Zhangmu.

They changed buses, cleared customs, met their Tibet Mountaineering Association 'minders' – Lawang, a Tibetan who had climbed the 8,200-metre Cho Oyu and who had come within a breath of the summit of Chomulungma as part of the successful 1975 Chinese Everest expedition; and Gao Lang Zi, a young Han Chinese working for the TMA in Lhasa, with good English, great sunglasses, but not a word of Tibetan.

They stayed at enormous expense in the dingy Hotel Zhangmu which was packed with tourists waiting for the roads ahead to clear. As happens so often, the route was blocked by landslides. The hotel restaurant, overlooking its precipitous rubbish dump, looked as if it could have taken flight at times itself.

They were glad to get moving again . . .

Dermot Somers's journal continues:

But tonight we skidded downhill into
Nyalam – a shoddy, provincial outpost, an
attempt at a Chinese town, or a garrison maybe,
botched on both accounts – grey and ugly with raw
concrete, iced-up streets, shuttered stalls,
institutional buildings.

There was a rash of pool halls, and a small,
neon-lit café where the rest of the expedition was
wolfing cabbage soup, vegetable stew, meat and
bamboo shoots, guzzling beer and plying chopsticks
in uncouth but effective styles. Our Nepalese
staff were already there demolishing rice and
sundries ahead of the rest, but the real host was
beaming, splay-toothed, Lawang, our Tibetan
liaison officer who hadn't a word of any language
we could approach at a shout but certainly
knew how to organise a good, international feed . . .

The following day, held up for nameless repairs to
buses, lorries, roads, weather, universe, we explored.
In the tedious way of climbers who could have spent
a useful day among the pool halls we
climbed surrounding hills instead, floundering
in deep snow, freezing winds and altitude pain
just above the chimney-height of the town. It was
a sobering experience and the pool halls might have
stood us in better stead.

ACCLIMATISING IN
THE LANGTANG
HIMAL, NEPAL. THE
SUN-SHADES BECAME
UMBRELLAS WHEN
THE WEATHER
BROKE. (FN)

(TOP) ENTERING OCCUPIED TIBET. (BOTTOM) POSSIBLY THE WORST BORDER HOTEL IN THE WORLD. NICK INFORMS JOHN THE COST IS $66 PER PERSON PER NIGHT.

That evening, Gao Lang Zi invited us to a dance.
With his flimsy blouson-style jacket slung over thin
shoulders, a casual scarf, jeans and innocently
affected English, he was the perfect 'townie',
drifting busily about his vague business, cigarette
in tremulous fingers, mediating in the purchase of
local goods. He was bitterly angry when our sherpas
bought some thermos flasks on their own initiative
and he abused them and their peasant culture roundly
to us. We explained gently and firmly that they were
our friends and colleagues, not our servants. Maybe
this left him without the role he had hoped for
himself.

But, detached eventually from his prejudices by
hardship, Gao was fine. He got on with us, and the
sherpas, and the Tibetans, without much fuss, and he
was as helpful as his taut temperament would allow.
It was a harsh posting for a sophisticated city boy
with a flair for languages and a desire to travel –
two dollars a day in the vast vacancy of the Rongbuk
glacier at 5,000 metres . . .

A military-style compound on the edge of town.
The social room was modelled on an Irish parochial
hall – who would have thought our style of decor could
be so far reaching? – painted in cream and drab-green
so the smoke and sweat wash off. A group of girls and a
bevy of boys stood apart, so stilted by each other they
were barely shocked at our arrival.

And we were a disgrace! The hall was cold, badly lit
with flammable crêpe around painted bulbs, and loud
with thin, mechanical pop which Gao told us with
satisfaction was the latest from the cultural capital.
We sat in a huddle in our duvets, balaclavas, hats,
and maybe even in some cases our mountain boots,
giggling and commenting as if we were superior beings
instead of a very uncouth and discomforting intrusion.

The locals ignored us correctly, and began to dance.
When I say 'locals', of course they were not Tibetans in
any proper sense: these were Chinese youth, second-
generation offspring of planters, bureaucrats and
military personnel.

They were good-looking people; tall, tough girls with a manner, who danced smoothly with each other, popping bubblegum without expression, their jeans well fitting and ersatz-trendy, while the sharp boys, who affected scarves and off-the-shoulder jackets, smoked stylishly, drank beer by the neck and danced companionably with each other, at a suitable physical distance. Occasionally the sexes joined up and did a languidly racy ensemble.

I left, out of embarrassment at our role; in true Irish style, all the innuendo was directed at the spectacle of males dancing together, and the hilarious implications if one of them asked one of us to dance! The worst feature of all that nonsense is the assumption that anyone would be even remotely interested in any of us, considering the state and the attitude of us . . . I believe we may have joined in later – but not without alcohol.

There is something forever haunting about the memory of those young Chinese expatriates – handsome, pretty – dancing coldly, smoothly together somewhere cheap and ordered within the desecrated wilderness of Tibet. They had the clockwork automation of the alien-born, moving like synchronised echoes to a chic music that is no longer theirs, in a foreign country that will never accept them; though they outnumber the Tibetans in many places they will always be strangers – outsiders imposed on the land by the rhythm of the machine-gun, and now imposing their disco-rhythms on a culture that is old enough and wild enough to have the anthem of its blood trapped forever within its own soil.

BRIEF SHADOW ON THE SNOW. (JM)

PREVIOUS PAGE:

FORTIFIED WALL AND MONASTERY, OVERLOOKING XEGAR, WAS DEVASTATED DURING THE CHINESE
CULTURAL REVOLUTION. FORTY YEARS LATER, THE MONASTERY HAS BEEN RE-OPENED. (JM)

❋ *Chapter 7* ❋

Caroline Doherty was feeling harassed. She'd been on the phone all morning trying to sort out flights for trekkers. Everything had been going well until Air India ran into industrial difficulties. The Indian ambassador in Dublin had been doing what he could.

Now a trekker was out on the shop floor looking for her. It had been like this for weeks – the same questions about shots, about visas, about boots and bags and gear . . .

Personal assistant to the managing directors of The Great Outdoors, Leslie Lawrence and Gerry Collins, she had been seconded to the expedition to handle the support treks. For the 38 people who had paid for a four-week holiday in Nepal and Tibet, it was a perfect arrangement; as it was for the expedition coffers, which would get 10 per cent of the take. Caroline was beginning to feel a bit like a tour guide, nursemaid and travel agent.

There were other problems. Even as the expedition left on St Patrick's Day, confirmation had not come through from Lhasa about the licence for the expedition's satpack. If all the gear barrels had gone missing, it couldn't have been worse. She was in daily contact with Margaret Stelfox in Belfast, who was finding it easier to make telephone and fax contact with both Nepal and Tibet. Margaret's familiarity with the situation was indispensable. She knew Bikram Neupane, the Nepalese trekking agent, from her own trips to Nepal, and Bikram had stayed in her house on a visit to Ireland. She had been to Lhasa and knew Gao Moxing in the Tibet Mountaineering Association. She was both efficient and persistent, and had a very understanding boss in her busy solicitor's office who had told her not to worry too much about the telephone bill.

She also had a very enthusiastic brother, Patrick Magennis, who could have been a very effective promoter if he hadn't decided to practise as a medical doctor. He was almost irrepressible in his efforts to raise funds. One of his latest had been to contact the Topographical Chocolate Company of Denver, Colorado, manufacturer of chocolate mountains; he had managed to persuade a courier company to deliver a substantial batch of 'Everest Easter eggs'.

Public interest, which has been aroused before the expedition's departure, had been stimulated by a wall poster for schools and by an *Irish Times* educational supplement, published in late March. By then, the first group of 12 trekkers were packing their rucksacks. Damien Cashin of The Call of the Wild was to take the first and third groups; the second, which included John Bourke, relief base camp manager, and relief doctor, Kathy Fleming, was to be led by his colleague, Tom Clear. Both Cashin and Clear were friends through the army reserve, the FCA.

The trekkers ranged in age and profession, from a student in her late teens to a nurse to two army chaplains and a retired civil engineer. Some were hardened hill-walkers and former climbers who regarded a trip to the Himalayas as a life-lasting experience. As if paying their way wasn't enough, a few threw their energies into packing food barrels, selling postcards and generally helping to raise funds. Valerie Burris, a former bank official who had enlisted with her husband, Maurice, for the second trek, even spent time organising visas in the Chinese embassy.

IRISH EVEREST TREK-
GROUPS AT BASE
CAMP (5,100M) ON
THE RONGBUK
GLACIER. (TOP) FIRST
TREK. (BOTTOM)
SECOND TRECK.

Back in Tibet, the expedition was on its way to the Rongbuk glacier, travelling by truck along the Friendship Highway through bleak, deserted Tibetan terrain. It was, Somers noted, like 'driving along the course of an irreparable earthquake, one from the deep core, where the ruin has been heavily silted and dusted over.'

The hills of Nepal are variously vegetated and usually farmed, but the Tibetan slopes seem stripped to their bare, loose understructure and best observed obliquely, in the distance. That may be a personal response – terrain as a symbol of tyranny – disregarding the ochres, terracottas, and umbers that colour no flag . . . In the land of the invader you are part of the invasion.

It is manifest in the children – poor, undernourished, grimy, sand-blasted, they stand back, whereas their counterparts in Nepal run riot in a celebration of uninhibited childhood. And the clandestine clamour for Dalai Lama photos among youths and men rife in 1987 is stilled now, as if that wave of optimism too had been silenced.

The convoy eventually approached Tingri, also known as Old or Lao Tingri, an historic trading post at 4,000 metres which is now base for an army camp. Here a farmer had opened his house up to serve yak butter tea and mommos or yakmeat balls, renaming it the Everest View Hotel. The tea was brewed with butter and soya in a tongma or large wooden cylinder which, one liaison officer had remarked, was used against the British in the military invasion led by Colonel Younghusband in 1904. Further down the road was Xegar or New Tingri, where, as in Zhangmu, the barrack-like Chomolungma Hotel with its cold water and leaking toilets charged western grade A rates.

A great stone spine, exposed, angular, ruined,
lifts up along the steep ridge above Xegar.
This is Xegardzhong, an historic walled monastery.
During the Cultural Revolution it was dive-bombed
by Chinese planes, strafed and ravaged as part of
the destruction of 3,000 monasteries throughout Tibet.

In 1987 we climbed up along its shattered length
and found, apart from desolation and slavering dogs
unchained, a small monastery reinstated with a
nucleus of monks and novices in the familiar saffron
robes. In settings like this it is tempting to
romanticise Buddhism as its humane abstractions offer
such an extreme alternative to the brutal excesses
of the Chinese system. But it should be remembered
too that institutionalised religion, operating as a
feudal system of control, was a deadweight on the
priest-ridden people of Tibet for centuries.

However, liberation from spiritual repression
can only come from within the human spirit,
not from military imperialism. The monastery in
Xegardzhong has further expanded now. Such
token Chinese gestures are visible throughout
the country. There is a tacit acknowledgment of the
savagery of the Cultural Revolution, and also of the
value of a little tourist-conscious liberalism. But
they are obviously aware too that every counter-
revolutionary stir begins in the monasteries.

Frank Nugent was an accomplished photographer. An arrangement had been made with *The Irish Times* to send back film whenever possible, and he had already despatched some rolls from the Langtang trek. He hadn't even had to wait till he got back to Kathmandu. A group of trekkers in Ghopte were delighted to oblige.

The lush rhododendron forests of the Langtang, the rickshaws and bookshops and fruitbats and commotion of Kathmandu, seemed a lifetime away now as the expedition convoy crested the 5,200-metre pass at Pang La, photographing the rainbow of prayer flags and the full Himalayan range beyond. They sang them out in the bitter wind – Makalu, Cho Oyu, Gyachung Kang, and Chomolungma itself, all bare brown rock and very little snow.

That snow was all around them. Base camp managers Leslie Lawrence and Nick Stevenson, Sherpas Jangbu and Khunke were already having problems, having gone ahead with gear in two lorries. The rest of the expedition was packed into a third truck, which disgorged every so often; walking sections would help to acclimatise.

Tumbling piles of mani stones bearing the Buddhist prayer to the lotus, *om mani padme hum*, signalled the village of Passum where they were to spend the night.

We had crossed the Pang La by now, the high pass that forms the first barrier before Everest, and although the Chinese wouldn't see it that way, we had left China behind and penetrated a genuine remnant of old Tibet. The vehicles had zigzagged up the expedition track to the rim of the pass while we staggered directly up for acclimatisation. Listening to the retching for air disguised as dry coughs, it was hard to believe this was a team honed for the summit of the earth.

Hard to believe either that the summit of the earth could be anywhere at hand. The land was even more like a burnt-out volcano covered in stones loosely held together by dust. But, from the windy rim of the pass, we beheld a haze of peaks on the horizon that could have been any height, any distance, if you didn't know Chomolungma, Cho Oyu. And of course we knew the tilted dolmen of Changtse standing out in front of Everest . . .

In the inner valleys, the road crawled through canyons, pastures, villages, river-beds. Where it suited the inhabitants, an irrigation dyke would slash across the track, and the lorries bucked and lurched in a frenzy of half-shafts. The houses are compact, tough, indigenous. Flat roofs, shuttered windows, self-sufficiency – brushwood fuel stacked upon the roofs and discs

'. . . A CULTURE OLD ENOUGH AND WILD ENOUGH TO HAVE THE ANTHEM OF ITS BLOOD TRAPPED FOREVER WITHIN ITS OWN SOIL'.

PRAYER-FLAGS
FLUTTER AS
BUDDHIST MONKS
FROM THE RONGBUK
MONASTERY
CONDUCT A
CEREMONY AT BASE
CAMP. (JM)

(TOP) FARMHOUSES HIGH IN THE RONGBUK VALLEY, CLOSE TO CHOMOLUNGMA. FUEL IS STACKED ON THE ROOF. (MM) (BOTTOM) IRISH BASE CAMP (5,100M), WITH THE BROWN MESS-TENT CENTRE, THE MEDICAL-TENT TO ITS RIGHT, AND THE BLUE KITCHEN-TENT IN THE FOREGROUND. THE MARQUEE AT THE REAR IS FOR CHINESE-TIBETAN STAFF (2). (JM)

of drying yak-dung plastered neatly on south-
facing walls. A fiercely rooted people, long
used to the raggle-taggle expedition trade.
Everest attempts have been trailing through here
for decades.

Lawang felt at home in Passum village, houses heated by the relentless sun. Here small children with matted hair, running noses, showed the mildest curiosity towards these westerners in their fleece tops and jeans, bearing 'designer' mountain gear. They were used to it. Passum's economy depended to a large extent on high altitude transport – the provision of herds of yaks for expeditions which had been approved by the Tibet Mountaineering Association. Lawang was rumoured to have been a village elder. He would use his influence, his contacts, to organise the expedition yaks. But the good people of Passum were to prove their worth to the Irishmen sooner than anticipated when the road became blocked with ice:

Just ahead, the valley threw out its arms
like the nave of a cathedral in awe before
Everest, and there in the flattening was the
Rongbuk monastery, the highest on earth; only
Buddhism could live that high, and probably
makes more sense here than it does in Dharmsala,
Berkeley, Ca., or at Hyde Park Corner.

 Nothing could stop us now. Everest towered in
front of us like a drive-in movie and the lorries
thundered towards it. Five of us had gone ahead
to scout the route to Base Camp – Dawson, Frank,
Dermot, Robbie, Mike . . . It came to us in a buzz
of happy conspiracy that we five had served our
dogged time together on Manaslu. An omen?

 The last time I had walked this ground, I was
going irreversibly down, through disastrous snow,
without the faintest notion of return. Now we
were back . . . in strength.

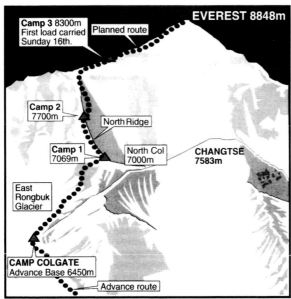

❊ *Chapter 8* ❊

'This is Wildtrack two to go with scene eight and scene nine.' Wind on a microphone; a child crying; yak bells; barking dogs. On 1 April, Brian Hayes and John Murray were up early, filming the sunrise over Xegar, directing the expedition lorry drivers to pass the cameras on the road. By the afternoon of the following day, they had arrived at Base Camp.

With some difficulty. The paperback, spiral-bound, expedition logbook recorded a more succinct version of events as they occurred on 17 April, when recalcitrant drivers hit their last river of ice. The entry had been filled in, neatly, with a black architect's pen:

Hired 15 Passum villagers + cleared ice + snow
from road, blocked in several places below Rongbuk
monastery. Cleared roads + arrived at Base
Camp approx 4 p.m.

Lawrence and Stevenson had stayed with the gear, making a bivouac with a tarpaulin, until the road could be cleared and it could be taken up. They were anxious to move. With the help of the Nepalese crew, led by sirdar (or foreman) Asha Rai, they had tents and barrels to organise.

Asha Rai was not to be confused with his namesake, and a partner with his employer, Nepal Trekhouse, known as Mr Rai. Dermot Somers wrote:

It may sound sanctimonious to say it,
but on this, our 'nth' trip to the Himalayas, we
didn't really have Nepali staff any more; we had a
team of friends and colleagues who were an integral
part of the Irish Everest expedition, and selected
on that basis.
    The agency with which we had worked since well
before Manaslu is Nepal Trekhouse, based
in the Patan area of Kathmandu at a
considerable distance from the droves jostling for
business in Thamel and Durbar Marg. Nepal Trekhouse
is run by two partners, Bikram Neupane – jovial,
sociable, focused – son of a High Court judge,
with a flair for personal relations and an eye for
detail – and Mr Rai, whose first name nobody knows.
    Mr Rai is a small, dignified, Nepali gentleman
from Darjeeling, who spent years in the British
Army stationed around the world. Later he
lived in Africa. His business career
began in the trekking and mountaineering field

OPPOSITE:

EVEREST NORTH FACE IN LEAN CONDITION. THE GREAT COULOIR IS IN THE SHADOW LEFT OF THE SUMMIT, AND THE HORNBEIN COULOIR IS ON THE RIGHT. (THE EAST RONGBUK APPROACH TO THE NORTH COL TURNS LEFT IN THE FOREGROUND.) (FN)

and goes back far longer than most of the present
crop of agents. They have close and valuable ties
with the very important Ministry of Tourism which
is responsible for mountaineering, and the very
volatile conditions that govern it.

We have established a relationship of mutual
trust with Bikram and Mr Rai which is essential
both in the delicate forward planning of an
expedition, and in the execution of detail in
conformity with ministry specifications.
Pre- monsoon '93 was an intense season for Nepal
Trekhouse; they had to handle two Everest expeditions
simultaneously – our North Ridge trip, and a
British 40th anniversary expedition to the south
side that was to put the first British woman on
top.

Asha Rai was the lithe, enthusiastic, exuberant sirdar who had been involved with some
of the climbers since the Manaslu expedition, when he had been sirdar to a trekking
group that followed them up to the newly opened Kali Gandaki valley. Afterwards, he
had worked with several smaller Irish trips, including one taken out by Somers to Island
Peak in 1992. The climber's diaries describe Asha then:

Asha is in his mid-30s, a small-framed,
energetic man who has survived in trekking
since he was an undersized adolescent living
on his wits. He speaks fast, humorous, utterly
demotic English and buzzes around at high speed
like a big outboard motor on a small boat.

Asha is not, properly speaking, a Sherpa. He
is Rai. The Rai people, of whom there are many
sub-divisions, live mainly in the Solu area,
slightly lower than the Sherpas who inhabit the
Khumbu, the well-known upland region reaching
the foot of Everest. Of course there are many
overlaps within this generalisation, including
the confusing tendency to call everyone a
'sherpa' anyway, with a small 's', regardless of
tribal origin.

The Sherpa people tend to dominate trekking
and mountaineering in Nepal, and it is a token

of Asha Rai's ability that he could be
appointed foreman on a complex expedition
operating in Tibet, where he had never been
before, when there were several experienced
Sherpas working with us as well. Much the
same really, as an Irish general foreman on
a British building site – he has to be that
much better than the competition.

A sirdar normally oversees the day-to-day
detail of an expedition – porters, loads,
campsites, meals; all the decisions apart
from those made by the climbers, though he
might have an advisory role here as well.
But this was a different kind of expedition,
lorries and yaks instead of porters, Chinese
and Tibetans loaded onto the decision process,
and our own specific Base Camp managers further
narrowing Asha's scope. He did an excellent
job, and one of the best measures of that
was the fact that you very rarely saw him do it.
In conditions of prolonged stress, where many
others would become fractious and over-
assertive, he helped to keep tension to a minimum.

We had several Sherpas, only one of whom was
hired as a 'high altitude porter' – that is, a
load-carrying climber high on the mountain.
There was a reluctance at the planning stage
to go the way of normal expeditions and staff
the attempt with experienced Sherpa climbers
whose job is to make the expedition a success
by whatever means are necessary. Of the 32
people who reached the summit from the simpler
south during one of our bleakest northside days,
at least 16 were paid Sherpas.

Our man in this role, hired at the last
moment, was Khunke Sherpa from Rolwaling. He
was the perfect choice. Enormously strong and
experienced, this was his eighth visit to the
north side of Everest. He had been high on
the mountain several times, but never to the
summit, and he had no ambition to go there,

(TOP) EAST RONGBUK
MORAINE AND ICE-
TOWERS. SUPPLIES
FOR ADVANCE BASE
CAMP.
(BOTTOM) ROUNDING
CHANGTSE ON THE
EAST RONGBUK.
EXHAUSTING
TERRAIN.

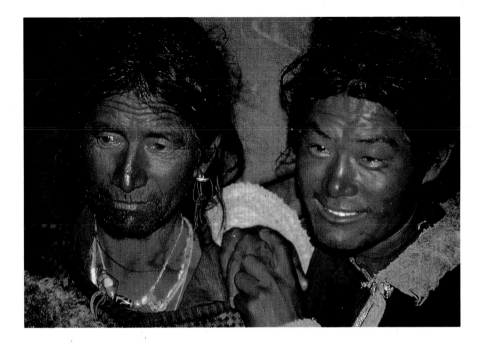

(TOP) TIBETAN YAK-
HERDERS. THE
EXPEDITION
DEPENDED ON THEIR
GOOD-HUMOURED,
ROBUST SERVICES.
(JM)
(BOTTOM)
HERDSMAN'S TENT
AND FODDER. (JB)

believing – correctly – that the North Ridge
is very dangerous with too much distance to
traverse and return at great altitude. Quiet
and self-contained, almost to the point of
taciturnity, he was courteous and undemanding
and moved like a machine on the mountain.

There was one most important piece of cargo which Leslie Lawrence had to assemble as
soon as he reached the snout of the Rongbuk glacier. It was packed into a robust little
box, weighing a mere 34 kilograms. He had already done a practice run back home.

For use in 'disaster relief, rescue, exploration and on scientific expeditions', the blurb
had said, describing how the 'satpack' could work in temperatures from minus 40 to plus
55°C, powered by a generator, and could transmit by an Inmarsat satellite stationed over
the Indian Ocean at 64 kilobits a second . . .

My newspaper was keen to start its regular coverage, and RTE's Pat Kenny was due
to make his first radio link-up with the expedition on reaching Base Camp at the end of
March. Come the first telephone link-up, on April Fool's Day, and there was silence. No
contact for the next 48 hours. The first *Irish Times* Everest log was due to be published
two days later.

Margaret Stelfox was philosophical on the phone from Belfast; there was no mention
of the difficulty in obtaining a permit from the Chinese. Back in Kathmandu a couple of
days later, there was a message from Lawrence for John Bourke who had just arrived with
the second trek from Ireland. Could he organise another generator?

A substantial Chinese-Taiwanese-Tibetan expedition was in the Rongbuk valley before
them. 'In before the bad weather clamped down,' Somers wrote:

> They were in the low base camp, at the bottom end of
> the Rongbuk site, and Lawang wanted us tucked in
> there with them – accessible, cosy, two liaison
> officers together in joint surveillance, like
> baby-sitters on shift work.
>   We disagreed. Every inch lower was an inch
> further whenever we went up. Doug Scott had used
> it in '87 and liked its grassy ambience and
> vegetarian milieu. Everything higher up was pure
> gravel-pit, but we were unconvinced.

There was an almighty row – the first, and perhaps the last, of its like. Lawang was
furious, waving his arms, shaking his head in a frenzy. The Irishmen were adamant. They
had been advised by other expeditions that the campsite tucked right underneath the

BREATHING LIFE
INTO THE AILING
GENERATOR.
O'NEILL-DEAN, LEFT,
EVEN FED IT OXYGEN
TO BOOST THE
POWER FOR
SATELLITE
BROADCASTS. (LL)

glacial moraine was the most sheltered place to be. After much shouting, the lorry driver
got into his cab. A decision had been reached, it seemed, and he was happy about it now.

Snow and gravel screeched beneath the
tortured tyres, the engine howled in labour –
we held collective breath. The roar mellowed,
settled to a throaty drone and the huge
machine waltzed delicately onto the plate
glass like a bull elephant ice-skating.
Overhead the chandelier of the sun chimed
and tinkled a warning. He never lost control,
never skidded or dipped; he let momentum,
profound grace, powerglide him to the other
side; and up on the moraine, as if clambering
out of evolution; a short stony skirmish
into the Irish Base Camp, with us racing
ahead, tossing our hats and cheering him
home and dry, like the first lorry to
break a siege.

(TOP) DESCENDING
FROM THE NORTH
COL (7,000M).
SAVAGE WINDS
SCOUR THE NORTH-
EAST RIDGE, LEFT.
(FN)
(BOTTOM) 'WHAT
THE —!' (JM)

(TOP) THE NORTH-EAST RIDGE LOOKS INNOCENT IN REPOSE. THE PINNACLES, TOP RIGHT. (JB) (BOTTOM) CHINESE-TAIWANESE CAMP (6,000M) AT THE FOOT OF THE NORTH COL. THE ROUTE FOLLOWS A DIAGONAL LINE ON THE RIGHT AND THEN BREAKS SHARPLY LEFT THROUGH THE UPPER ICE-CLIFFS. (FN)

He barrelled out of the
cab, a big, shaggy, Genghis Khan in a
leather overcoat that may have had the
fangs and claws still on it, and shook
hands with us each in turn. You
could see he would have hugged
us – but Irishmen don't go in for that
sort of thing.
      As the commotion died down, we gazed
around, and recognised every bleak
extrusion of the place, unchanged as one's
own scars on a hungover morning . . . Base
Camp, God help us – The Boys were back in
town.'

There were 16 small dome tents for 16 bodies, 16 sets of gear, one large mess tent provided by the army, a smaller medical tent, four Sherpas' tents, and a large khaki-coloured heavy canvas tent for Lawang and Gao: it looked very cheerful. It was even more so when, with much humming, cymbals, chanting, the monks from Rongbuk bedecked Base Camp with prayer flags and blessed all who slept there with a symbolic casting of flour to the mountain winds.

On 5 April, Day 20 in the still relatively pristine logbook, the campers were happy to hear a familiarly discordant, comforting, alpine sound: the bells of 40 yaks, arriving to take gear up the Rongbuk glacier to Advance Base – the 6,450-metre-high Camp Colgate, named gratefully, and without a cringe, after the main sponsor.

Lawrence was feeling relaxed. After some haggling over a hike in yak prices, the group had weighed the blue barrels and followed the yaks on the 12-mile haul up to 6,450 metres – 400 metres higher than originally estimated when examining the maps back at home. He was thinking of the evening meal that the cook, Aka Raj, would produce in the near-deserted Base Camp when he heard that there was a phone call for him at the Chinese camp.

Back in *The Irish Times* office in Dublin, Qiang Zhao, a Chinese postgraduate student in civil engineering, was trying to save this reporter's life. He had taken a morning off from his study of water quality in Dublin Bay to write a fax in neat Chinese characters on *Irish Times* notepaper.

Nails bitten to the quick, dodging behind my desk any time I caught sight of the features editor, I had decided to contact the Tibet Mountaineering Association in Lhasa to see if it had any information.

We didn't need to transmit the message. Caroline Doherty relayed a number for the Chinese expedition's satellite phone, on which Lawrence had called her that morning. A woman's voice at the other end told me in broken English to ring back; 20 minutes later, there was a breathless Lawrence, coughing uncontrollably. He didn't sound too pleased. No one could blame him. He had just managed to get his own satpack working, at last.

At least his journey wasn't in vain. He could always nip into the Chinese toilet on the way back up to Base Camp. To Somers, himself a skilled and discerning builder, the crude structure was symbolic:

> There was one feature, and we couldn't miss it on the way in. In the centre of this natural amphitheatre, this compound composed equally of barren geology and bleak space, overshadowed by the highest north face on the planet, the Chinese had erected a toilet block. Square, solid and ugly as a monument to totalitarian faith.
>
> Built of rugged granite, it has slots in the floor, sloped at the wrong angle into an open pit behind. The north wind howls up through these holes, even on a day when there is no wind blowing at all. We had to invent a means of dealing with paper. A simple engineering solution on which we prided ourselves. We left a large tin trunk in the toilet block, complete with windproof lid, to contain used paper, and burn it at intervals.
>
> Within hours, the box had disappeared, leaving a sense of outrage, almost sacrilege, behind it – and its contents scattered widely. It took some lateral thinking to piece together the meaning . . .
>
> The ornate tin trunk, part of our baggage, was worthless to us, but it was obviously worth a great deal in the upland culture of the Rongbuk. It must have seemed gratuitously insulting that we would use such a valuable object for containing, of all things, used toilet paper in a society that doesn't even *use* toilet paper, which is the quintessential consumer product; and these are third-world people who have made a creative virtue of living off the discarded wrappings of consumerism.

Robbie Fenlon was back in Base Camp. Altitude had got the better of him on the first trek up the glacier to Advance Base, and he had taken a wise decision to retreat, recover and try again. Resuscitating with a tin mug of hot lemon tea and a bowl of creamed rice, he was happy enough to talk when I made contact again the following week on the phone.

It was, he said, a fair old shock to the system. He had been feeling 'pretty dire' by the time they had reached the first overnight camp. At 5,700 metres, it had taken some of them three hours to get out of the tents.

Whatever about feeling dire, Dermot Somers and Richard O'Neill-Dean felt little better when they arrived back in his pursuit. On reaching Advance Base, the pair began to get worried when there was no sign of him. They were concerned that he was too ill to move and was stuck somewhere. Accompanied by Khunke bearing emergency gear, they almost ran down parts of the glacier. The extraordinary effort knocked both of them out for days.

Fenlon seemed bemused, unaffected by their concern. This was his manner, often disarming. At times he seemed to ooze confidence. It was apparent in an interview to camera on the way in. 'There was no question then,' he had said simply. 'I mean if there was an Irish Everest expedition going, I had to be on it. And there was no apprehension at all about it, no second thoughts, no wondering should I be on this or should I not.'

Those who knew him could smile. He was as unsure, as apprehensive, as anyone. Yet he was secure enough to be able to laugh at his own human condition.

'I mean, the only thing you can see is your feet, the only thing you can feel is your breathing,' he said of his first retreat. 'You become absolutely wasted . . . you feel no energy levels at all and you can't think. You're just this sort of flesh machine trying to move through the landscape and you're doing a bad job.'

Nevertheless, he was disappointed. 'Walking up there . . . it feels like the hardest thing you've ever done in your life . . . It was like turning my back on the mountain and I sort of felt, well, if this is the way it's going already, it's a bad omen.'

Young Tony Burke had continued up to Advance Base Camp; apart from a slight headache, a little dizziness on the second day, a loss of appetite, he felt 'reasonably well'. His experience of altitude had been limited to Mont Blanc up till now. Base Camp itself was higher than he had ever been before.

He spoke in clipped sentences, preferring to use the third person and rarely referring to himself. Hayes pushed him a little for the film:

'At any stage, do you feel so bad that you say "ah, shag it, this isn't really worth it"?'

'No . . . that thought can cross one's mind, yes, you can sort of think "what am I doing here?" But the overall goal totally outweighs the physical condition . . . It's a question of having patience, of riding through the physical and mental storms when one increases in altitude.'

The climbers and four of the Nepalese staff – Jangbu, Khunke, Doarjee and Dendi – worked on establishing the second camp. It was a bleak spot, just below the North Col,

PREVIOUS PAGE:

ON TO THE NORTH
COL (7,000M).
BEWARE THE
SUDDEN DROP. AT
THIS POINT WE
TURNED SOUTH FOR
CHANGTSE, 1987 –
NORTH FOR EVEREST,
1993. (JM)

with leaden clouds and the shadow of the mountain stealing the warmth of the morning sun. George Leigh Mallory had missed this approach by the East Rongbuk glacier to the north face of the mountain on his first trip with Howard-Bury's expedition in 1921.[1]

Even the title – Advance Base – was misleading; for early American expeditions, it was Camp Three. Stelfox was willing to admit to much suffering in the first few days.

'It's high, it's getting up into the reaches, it's beyond the level where you can indefinitely stay. Nobody is doing too much. We've got the camp established, we've got our mess tent fairly well sorted out, but you need two or three days just sitting around to get used to it before you can really even think about going further.'

How did it feel to be 'sucking for oxygen', as Brian Hayes described it?

'Well, the coughing and spluttering is part of it . . . you've got to work a lot harder just to think about things, can't move as fast, everyday things like putting on your clothes, making a cup of tea, tying your shoe laces, everything takes an awful lot more thought and concentration of effort.'

They would be going back down to Base Camp again, as part of the sleep-low-climb-high strategy associated with the 'siege' method of ascent. Then they would feel better, he said. But it would take patience and time.

'It's not even a progression, you don't necessarily get better day by day. Yesterday I felt a lot better than I do now. I'm fairly well drained of energy. Yesterday I was able to hump stones and throw barrels around and get things organised . . . even think about writing a letter. Today, I can't do very much.'

On 9 April, the evening radio call from Base Camp reported that the first group of trekkers had arrived, with post and papers and news from home. Up at Advance Base, Stelfox and Nugent decided to visit their Chinese and Taiwanese neighbours; a small but very independent Korean expedition was also present. The Chinese team had been well-equipped back down at Base with two land cruisers, a 2,000-watt generator, full fluorescent lighting in their army tents. Lawrence had decided – for absolutely no reason – that the one woman among the Chinese group had to be the manager's secretary.

It was a useful meeting in the mess tent, a dismembered goat in the corner, green tea on the brew. The Chinese were about ten days ahead of the Irish in their staged ascent. It was agreed that the two teams should co-operate: the Chinese would allow the Irish to use the ropes they had fixed in place up to the North Col. In return, the Irish would carry up some of the Chinese gear.

Time-consuming and expensive, the practice of using fixed ropes tends to be confined to big mountains. By this system, the sections of the route need only be climbed once. After that, they are protected by a fixed line which allows for quick and safe passage, using jumars and karabiners.

On 10 April, Fenlon, Somers and O'Neill-Dean set off from Base Camp to move back up the glacier. At nine o'clock the following morning, Stelfox told Lawrence that six climbers and two sherpas expected to go up the North Col with light loads, the first step towards establishing Camp One.

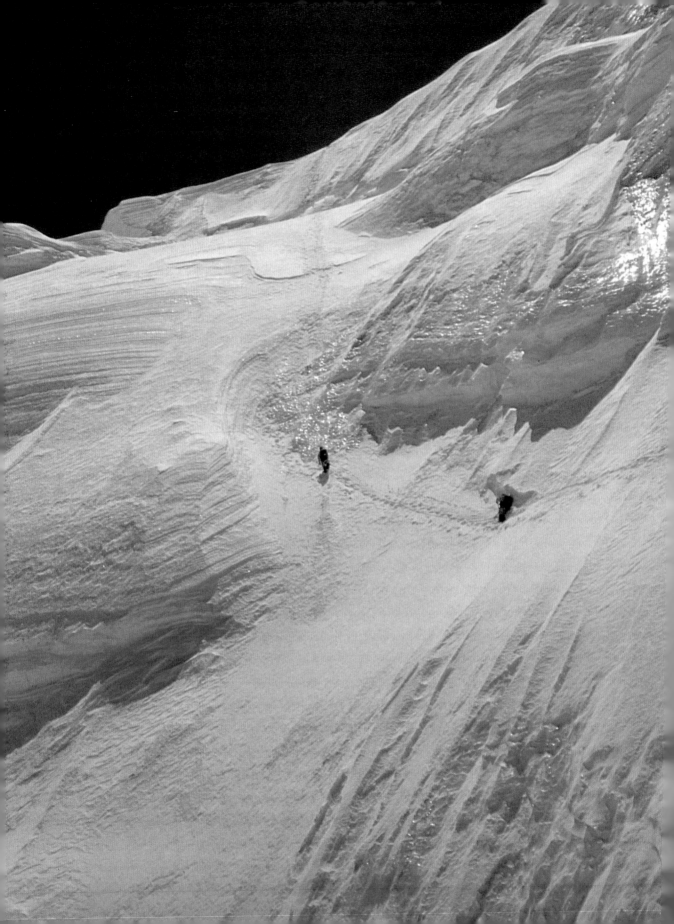

Formed by a steeply falling glacier, the 500-metre vertical wall of snow and ice up to the saddle, linking Everest to Changtse, is one of the most dangerous sections of the northern route. Yet the climbers would spend more time here than on any other section, relentlessly hauling gear to the higher camps. Mallory had not been too impressed with it, or with his breakfast, when he had pitched his tent up there on the narrow ledge in 1922 – then the highest point that man had ever camped. His tea was almost undrinkable, because the water 'boiled' at tepid temperature at such an altitude. His tins of spaghetti had frozen solid.

Four or five paces. Collapse. Recover again. Stelfox was weary, but wary. With its risk of avalanche, the North Col approach had claimed many lives. Nugent and Barry were below him, Khunke was disappearing into the distance ahead. Every time he stopped, Dawson was racked by persistent coughing – 'almost vomiting with the intensity of it,' he wrote:

It's nearly noon and a powerful sun in a
cloudless sky has turned the early morning
crust into a sticky stodge, sucking power
from already feebled legs and draining will.
There is no escaping the sun on these open
slopes, reflected off the surface and focused
by the flanking walls. High above, a precarious
overhanging serac threatens our slow passage
across its path, for sooner or later it will
come down, bringing with it thousands of tons
of snow and the tangle of old ropes threaded
improbably through its icy core . . .

Good intentions are destroyed by lassitude.
Breakfast was the usual ordeal – taste and
appetite ruined by altitude. Conversation
was sparse, someone threw up outside . . .

Frank and Mike are getting close . . . Mick
and Tony not far behind . . . got to keep
moving. Up to the next rope. Jumar on,
back up, karabiner on, plod on, and on. Halfway
up now, a broad platform and obvious place
for a rest. Coughing and choking for some
minutes.

When I can look up, Khunke is halfway across
the long traverse that leads out left to the
bottom of a steep ice pitch. Above and beyond
him the North Ridge is in view, snow merging

OPPOSITE:

STEP ICE LEADS TO THE NORTH COL. LOAD-CARRYING REQUIRED MANY TRIPS ON THIS GROUND, THREATENED BY ICE-CLIFFS KNOWN AS SERACS. CONDITIONS HERE VARIED FROM SEVERE COLD TO UNCOMFORTABLE HEAT. (FN)

into rock, the skyline summit ridge a long,
long way above.

Time slips by and I have to move. Across
the traverse and onto the steep ground,
camera out as the drama of the situation
penetrates a brain focused on pain. The
ice pitches demand a new rhythm – a steady
plod no use here; short bursts of power
interspersed with long slumps in the harness . . .

The angle eases and the
bergschrund, the last barrier to the Col,
appears, bridged by a short aluminium
ladder skewered into the snow with aluminium
stakes.

Crampons squealing on the metal rungs,
one step at a time, up the steep ice beyond
and suddenly the snow is falling away below
and I'm looking across the West Ridge into
Nepal. Up, over and one leg astride the ridge
to pause and marvel at the position . . .

A hundred metres to go, and even the gentlest
of slopes forces a halt and a desperate
search for strength. The Col appears – four
Chinese tents, a small legacy of broken poles
and rubbish, and Khunke, smiling, relaxed,
handing me a cup of tea. Load off, and lying
in the snow, spent but satisfied, first time
to 7,000 metres for me, first time to
the North Col and suddenly . . . pleasure surpassed
the pain and this altitude thing doesn't seem so
bad after all . . .[2]

❋ *Chapter 9* ❋

13 APRIL – Somers, O'Neill-Dean carried Chinese loads to North Col. Korean, Mr Hu (37 years) and Sherpa left at 5 a.m. for summit but no contact by radio until last night, battery low?

Lawrence's log entries had been reduced to a scrawl. He'd also been exercising his vocal chords. The following day, temperature minus 10°C, the Nepali staff and six of the climbers were back down with him at Base Camp for the trekkers' farewell dinner.

Nick Stevenson and Stephen Potts were leaving, as arranged, with the first trek: John Bourke and Kathy Fleming, the second team doctor, would arrive with the second trek to relieve them. As Somers and O'Neill-Dean put in lonely load-carrying hours up the mountain, there was some news from the Koreans. Mr Hu and his Sherpa had reached the summit shortly after lunchtime on 13 April and had descended . . . without any permit, by Nepal!

They were like ghosts on the mountain, these extraordinary summiteers, their presence entirely unreal to the Irish still struggling with altitude on the lower slopes. They were arrested in Nepal. Illegal entry!

Rongbuk was getting busy. A German expedition arrived to climb the 7,000-metre peak, Dong Fang, followed by a Swiss group of eight – a commercial trip rather than an expedition, for each of them had paid about 12,000 US dollars for the opportunity. Dr Kathy Fleming would get to know them very well; within a few days of setting up camp, one of the Germans had to be evacuated with pulmonary oedema.

00873-1447361. 00873-1447362. Martin Stubbs, head of the British Meteorological Office's central forecast office (CFO) in Bracknell, Berkshire, was a little perplexed. He had dialled both numbers, one a fax, one a phone, repeatedly. There was no response. Perhaps the generator wasn't on?

It was through John Bourke that the arrangement had been made with Stubbs to send regular long-term weather reports to the Irish group by the satpack's fax from the third week in April. Stubbs was also helping out the British 40th anniversary expedition on the Nepalese side of the mountain. It was an interesting exercise for his forecasters – a change from airports and planes.

As one of two weather centres providing worldwide information for aviation, Bracknell draws data from a network that includes the Irish Meteorological Service, Stubbs had told me by phone for an *Irish Times* report. Gathered twice a day, that data was gobbled up and ascribed to some 1.25 million grid points all over the world within three-and-a-half hours of the observations being made; forecasts were extrapolated by a computer carrying out 800 million instructions a second; predictions for six days ahead were printed out within a mere 40 minutes . . .

Tibet was an area of 'poor data coverage', with few, if any, meteorological observation stations and upper air stations over the barren Himalayan region. The forecasters had to assist the computer by examining satellite photographs, taken by the

US polar orbiter which covers every point on the globe twice a day. Despite all this new technology, the 24-hour and 48-hour forecasts of wind and temperature at three altitudes – 5,400, 7,000 and 9,000 metres respectively – could only give 'general information', Stubbs emphasised. Local conditions could – and would – vary quite a lot.

He wouldn't be around to hear the outcome. He was off on a month's holiday to Pakistan, but would wave as he crossed the Himalayas by plane. Within a week, I would also be flying out with the third trek, bearing rucksack, daysack and a laptop computer, wrapped in a space blanket for temperature change . . . and altitude!

'Is bearna mór é, an North Col. Is balla mór oighre é . . . chomh luath agus is féidir, tosnóimíd ar an dreapadóireacht.'

Somers, fluent Irish speaker, was talking to Murray and Hayes at Camp Colgate, for the Irish version of the film. Camp One was now well stocked with food, cookers, gas. Further up, the Chinese and Taiwanese had postponed a summit bid due to heavy snow. Pulling back, they had lost some equipment when a fire broke out in one of their tents. They wanted to borrow three oxygen masks.

It was on 25 April that Camp Two was put in place at 7,700 metres (25,025 feet) – 100 metres higher than originally planned, according to the status report compiled by John Bourke. Five days before, Nugent, Barry and Dendi had carried loads to 7,500 metres. Stelfox, Somers, O'Neill-Dean, Fenlon and Khunke had continued the carrying, but had returned to the North Col to sleep for the weather was less than pleasant.

It was snowing spasmodically, and there were biting 25 to 40-knot winds which hammered against the tents and made it difficult to sleep. 'Khunke shot off in front up the broad snow crest of the ridge, but the going was firm and windswept and we all made good time, leaving the snow and up the broken rocky spur to a small exposed platform at 7,700 metres,' Stelfox wrote. 'We erected one tent, stashed our loads and scurried down to the relative comfort of Camp One . . .'

They had left four tents, four stoves, some oxygen, some gas. There was a sense of relief as they descended after seven hours of trail-breaking, fresh snow enveloping them, hard snow on the route. At worst, Camp Three could always be set up on the way to the summit, but there could be no movement without Camp Two.

They would go right back down the Rongbuk again to recover, leaving Nugent, Barry, Burke and Murphy at Advance Base to keep the momentum going – siege-style mountaineering, climbing high, sleeping low and setting camps progressively. Dendi was a little bemused. He had been a high-altitude Sherpa until he had sustained injuries in a motorbike accident. He was meant to be cook on this trip but had voluntarily handed kitchen duties over to his mate, Dhana. Of Dhana, Dermot Somers wrote:

In 1993, Dhan Bahadur Rai, cook at Camp Colgate, was 22 years old, resident poet and musician, full of delicacy and affection, with a diligent sense of subjunctive grammar, the whole paragon no more than five foot tall.

OPPOSITE:

(TOP) SUNSET AGITATES THE WEATHER. CHINESE TENTS ON THE NORTH COL (7,000M). (JM) (BOTTOM) TOWARDS CAMP TWO. WIND-BLOWN CLOUD AND SNOW STREAM FROM THE SUMMIT. (JM)

His kitchen was a stone enclosure roofed at crouching height with a tarpaulin. Dhana saw himself flitting perpetually about the place to feed us; he wrote a poem in Nepali, translated to English, 'Who are you, o Phedi-bird?', in which he compares himself to a familiar bird that nests in stone walls and flies in and out with food. He composed two expedition songs celebrating the Irish experience on Sagarmatha/Chomolungma and the cultural bond between Nepal and Ireland, a link he has in many ways enhanced.

Dhana was reared in a remote Rai community high in the mountains of Solu, a week's walk from the Nepali side of Everest. His culture is in decline, his language a minority tongue. Nepali, the national language, is silencing the ancient voices of the hills. In his high homeland on the fringe of Khumbu, the dominant race are the Sherpas and, though there isn't a caste system in Nepal, as there is in India, discrimination is endemic.

Born to illiterate parents, a large family, a tiny farm, Dhana was destined to be a goatherd. As a child on a wordless mountainside, he would hide behind bushes and watch another boy turn strange pages. At the age of ten, a Sherpa farmer punished him wrongly for damaging crops. There was no redress. He was seized by a helpless anger at his own plight. He stayed awake all night, ten years old, and planned to escape from ignorance.

Education was feared in his community, but Dhana put himself through school and into university with a decade of such effort that it can only be dimly grasped by reference to the relentless geography from which he came.

Living in remote school-villages on nothing but aspiration, he traded sugar-cane from home for single pages. He learned to speak Nepali fluently, and to write it with the hand of an artist. He came first, second, or third in every class, for which there was a scholarship of a few pence a month.

He studied Euclidean geometry and Newtonian physics in schools surrounded by the animistic culture of the hill-people, for whom he has enormous respect, having intuited the transparency of the new world.

He learned music too and found a natural aptitude for instruments. He brought home everything he learned. His brothers and sisters are following his direction. Dhana says that the value of education lies in the expansion it brings to impoverished lives. He is training to be a teacher in order to help that process.

College life is expensive and he subsidises it with work on trekking trips and expeditions. He has worked almost exclusively with Irish groups in the past few years.

When the farm was sub-divided recently, according to custom, among all the sons, Dhana re-arranged it and gave a share to his elder sister. There is a struggling school now, run by the community. It had no playground, as a Sherpa farmer owned the land up to the four walls. Dhana has given a plot of his own land to the farmer on condition that the school has a playground outside its door.

Leslie Lawrence was on the VHF. The Chinese had given the Swiss group permission to use their fixed ropes to the North Col for the sum of 1600 US dollars. The Swiss would be leaving base the following day.

'They're a fairly lively lot, and they're working under time constraints,' he told Nugent. 'They want to get in and out fairly quickly so they are going to be running up and down those ropes like monkeys, I should think. Over.'

'Ah, they still have to breathe in and out through their noses like everyone else,' Nugent laughed. He was concerned about other things. Four yaks had arrived up for the Chinese, bearing a dried hind of yakmeat, eggs and cigarettes for their climbers.

'They seem to have a very active base camp down there . . . people were saying that it's an awful pity we don't have that sort of organisation. I said, of course, that's totally unfair and totally untrue and we *know* that you know the local butcher.'

Lawrence picked him up. Of course he would send a barrel full of goodies – eggs, chocolate and even some fags for Mike Barry – with the Swiss. He had never realised his fondness for yakmeat stew.

Jangbu Sherpa would not hear the news for some days, but there was trouble over the other side of the hill. On 28 April, the Kathmandu English newspaper, *The Independent*, reported that his 32-year-old sister-in-law, Pasang Lhamu Sherpa of Solu had 'fulfilled her life's dream', becoming the first Nepali woman to reach the summit of Sagarmatha, the Nepali word for Everest. The fact that she was leader, and that she had brought five of her compatriots with her, was another record, the newspaper noted. It was the largest number of Nepalis on the world's highest point at any one time.

Regrettably, however, Pasang's magnificent achievement has been overshadowed by a thick pall of gloom, the report read. 'Indeed, as this is being penned five days after her moment of glory, it would appear that she and her colleague, Sonam Tshiring Sherpa of Dolakha, may have perished sometime after having bivouacked on the south summit on their descent.'

Pasang Lamu was also the daughter of a colleague of Bikram Neupane. Exhilaration could not substitute for exhaustion: statistically, Everest claimed many more lives on the descent.

Somebody had picked up *The Ascent*, a mountaineering thriller by veteran Himalayan climber, Jeff Long, on the way out. 'Ten men and two women on the brink of the abyss', its subtitle had promised. The first chapter's account of the slow death of a woman buried alive in the mountains of Wyoming had certainly delivered on that. It had everything – climbing as politics, as religion, even a bit of sex too. One wondered about this bit: weeks of greasy hair, dried burnt skin, cracked fingertips, racking coughs were better than any contraceptive. Thermals, fleeces, duvets were fairly sexless garments at the best of times, but if one had not changed one's socks . . .

Peeing into a plastic bottle within the confines of a sleeping bag – the men's little

(TOP) CELEBRATING THE SUCCESSFUL CHINESE/TAIWANESE /TIBETAN EXPEDITION ON 5 MAY 1993, WITH THE EXPEDITION LEADERS AND THE PRESIDENT (SECOND FROM LEFT) OF THE TIBET MOUNTAINEERING ASSOCIATION. (JM)

(BOTTOM) 'SO . . . WHAT IS THE PLAN?' THE PRE-SUMMIT MEETING OF 5 MAY AT BASE CAMP. (JM)

'luxury' – and constantly boiling little pots of snow was becoming a bit of a drag. It was such a tonic to return to Base Camp, to absorb the heat of the sun in the mornings and to live again. A chess set had been put together from a selection of small stones; Bourke and Fleming were eager pupils of the poker school, with Stelfox as treasurer handing the Chinese Foreign Exchange Coupons or FECs.

Robbie Fenlon had been doing his bit for the film crew. 'As a climber, what does the North Col mean to you?' Hayes asked him.

'To me, it's just a staging post,' said Fenlon. 'Other people seem to be fascinated by the views, but I still feel that the whole thing of the altitude gives you tunnel vision, and you just get up there and you can start to feel the altitude coming on, so it's a place I feel like getting out of fairly quickly. The ropes are fixed on it. So it's not a technical challenge. Altitude is what we are climbing here. Not technical difficulty.'

On 2 May, the last of the Chinese loads were carried to Camp Two, and Frank Nugent and Tony Burke spent the first night there with Khunke and Dendi. Nugent's lips were badly split and bleeding, his hair seemed to have gone white, his face was ravaged by the mountain sun.

It would be the first of three nights that Burke would spend there with different partners, melting pots of snow and listening to Talking Heads, Enya and the Choirboys on his Walkman. He was particularly proud of the fact that he hadn't washed or changed his clothes for about five weeks. He and Nugent chatted about their chances of moving up to Camp Three at 8,300 metres the next morning. The expedition schedule had pencilled in the establishment of this top camp on Mayday, leaving another eight days for stocking before making a summit attempt.

The night was uncomfortable, their bubble tent was buffeted about, and they were driven down the following morning by 70-knot winds. The Chinese expedition reported that they had lost a tent at their third camp, a little further up, but they were sticking it out. They intended to make a push and had actually named a date.

Despite foul conditions, six of them – four Tibetans, one Chinese and one Taiwanese – succeeded on 5 May, but at a price. The four Tibetans made it back to the North Col, but the Chinese and Taiwanese were reported to be 'out of radio contact'.

Advance Base was deserted. There had been an obvious break in the settled weather, and so everyone had come back down to base for The Meeting. It was informal, sitting around on stools, sipping coffee or Apeel orange juice from tin mugs. But it would determine the future of the expedition, and it was being filmed. Dawson, as leader, was in The Chair, which was a fairly uncomfortable camping stool.

They had roughly three weeks of 'comfortable time' before they'd have to think about packing up and heading off, he said. Past experience indicated that the next ten days to a fortnight would offer a settled spell of weather. 'So really, next time we go up from here, that's going to be our chance of going to the top . . .'

It was totally open, nothing was set or certain, he stressed. 'I think it is up to everybody to be as honest as they can be about their own state, ambitions, commitments . . .'

Dawson wanted to formulate a plan; Dermot was reluctant, preferring to take each day as it came. Nugent rowed in to support the leader, and mentioned the figure of 'two'.

Silence. The leader broke it again. There were certain advantages in trying to get several people up at once, he said. There were two options: selection by consensus of those two, three or four; or movement up in two groups, postponing a decision until the third camp was well in place. In any case, Khunke, as the leading high-altitude Sherpa, would have to have a chance to have a rest.

Dawson was aware that he and Frank had already been recommended. He had to clear the air. 'Tony has very kindly singled out Frank and me as two people . . . I mean, I don't see that that's as clear-cut by any means as that. I would think that it is necessary for people to come out now and say at this stage whether . . . how strongly they feel that they are going to be going well enough and have the commitment to go to Camp Three and to the summit.'

'Now maybe that's very difficult to say that sitting down here in the sunshine, but I think that it is necessary for people to be honest about it, because we all came out here with the idea that it would be possible for any one of us, two of us or whatever, to get to the summit, and I certainly don't want to be starting to rule out anybody's chances at this stage.

'I would much prefer if people ruled themselves out . . . I think most people are physically healthy but I think it's very much the commitment – to want to put the effort in – which will make the difference.'

He appealed again: 'If people haven't made the decision, it's fair enough, but if people have made the decision one way or the other, whether to be in support or whether they would like to be going for the summit, I think people should say that.'

He declared his hand. 'I'll start and say that I would like to go to the summit . . . if I'm physically able when I get up there. But at the same time if there are other people who are going better than me, I'm quite prepared to support them.'

Another pause, and then it was Tony Burke. He would like to go to the summit as well, but felt that Nugent was in much better condition. He had seen it during their time up at Camp Two.

The leader had put the carrot out, Mick Murphy observed: 'I'd be quite prepared to support somebody going to the summit as long as I got a chance to go myself afterwards. I'm determined to have my own try for the summit no matter what, but I support the first team to go there by carrying whatever's necessary, and to come down for a day or two and have a go myself afterwards.'

The summit was 'the most important thing', Mick continued. Personal ambitions came second. 'So I think other people might think like that too . . .'

There was much shuffling of feet; no one replied. Frank tried to ease the tension: 'This is a bit like Alcoholics Anonymous.'

'Well, I've had a good long rest and I'm feeling very fit,' said Dermot. 'And I'm looking forward to starting back up tomorrow if that's the way it works out. And I think that those of us who go up tomorrow will be starting to work, to set things up, not necessarily for ourselves.

'You know what my ideas on plans are, and I'm certainly sceptical as to how any blueprint that we lay out will fulfil itself. I simply think that we go up, the group of us that are prepared to go . . .'

Tony Burke intervened. 'But we can't really waste time, we can't procrastinate with the weather.'

There was some further discussion. While some wrestled with their emotions, Mike Barry's approach was purely practical. It would be ridiculous, in his view, to expect a summit team to carry to Camp Three. They should conserve their energies, and leave that work for the support. He was seeking a decision there and then.

> One glimpse and it draws you, beckons you, pulls
> you in. It was just the peak at first, snow-capped,
> with its distinctive little plume of cloud. Then, as
> we trudged across the brown, barren boulder moraine
> in silence – boot upon rock, boot upon snow and
> ice – Everest opened out at last against a deep
> blue Tibetan sky. It had taken two weeks to make
> it, but then covering the Irish Everest expedition
> is no ordinary reporter's marking . . . [1]

After a week's freedom from the daily grind of news markings, it had been difficult enough to focus the mind on work, never mind think of some sort of half-decent introduction to a report. A week's acclimatisation trek in the Langtang had had a very disarming effect.

Fresh images of juniper, gentian, rampant rhododendron, queueing for ice-cold washes under the village tap, had kept us going as we moved from the climatic patchwork of lush green Nepal into Tibet at the beginning of May.

Mr Wang, Chinese liaison officer for the third trek, had been full of information as he travelled in the front seat of one of the land 'scriptures', his name for the sturdy four-wheel drives. He had heard about England's 'liberation' of Ireland, and knew that the Republic had many volcanoes. 'Iceland?' we said tentatively, but it seemed to pass him by.

His jovial mood had changed at Xegar or New Tingri when we met up with Rory McKee in the Chomolungma Hotel. Rory was having problems with altitude and had spent the best part of a week there, reading and walking up the road and back again. He was relieved to see us, and was looking forward to a lift back to Base Camp. Mr Wang and the four drivers had other ideas. It took 100 US dollars for them to change their minds.

Over lunch at the Rongbuk monastery on our final approach, the young monks wanted to show us their altar to the Dalai Lama, decorated with packets of biscuits, flour,

(TOP) MURRAY MEDIA
– JOHN MURRAY AND
JANGBU FILMING ON
THE NORTH COL.
(MB)
(BOTTOM) SIGI
HUPFAVER, VETERAN
OF EVEREST AND
SEVEN OTHER
SUCCESSFUL 8,000-
METRE ASCENTS,
WITH MEMBERS OF
THE GERMAN
EXPEDITION TO
DONG FANG (7,018M)
VISITING BASE CAMP.

TWO CLIMBERS ON
THE NORTH RIDGE
WITH CAMP ONE ON
THE NORTH COL
VISIBLE IN THE
DISTANCE. THE
EXPEDITION ROUTE
APPROACHED FROM
THE RIGHT AND
REACHED THE
NORTH COL, NEAR
THE TENTS. (RF)

bags of dried fruit juice and other 'expedition souvenirs'. Mr Wang was keen to give his version of events. The obvious destruction to the building had been the result of 'too many tourists', he asserted. 'Too many visitors, all wanting to take bricks.'

Aka Raj, the cook, had the water on as we picked our way across a patch of frozen glacier, tramped across the arid plain, gasped at the mountain opening out in front of us with only a wisp of cloud veiling its features. Some of the trekking group shed a few tears; others were busy identifying Changtse, the North Ridge and the famous yellow band of limestone at over 8,000 metres.

It had taken him some five decades to get there, but Brendan Henshaw, a retired engineer with the Government's Office of Public Works, had been reading, eating, sleeping Everest for years. Like many of these trekkers, his knowledge about the Himalayas was encyclopaedic.

I had my 'bible', a paperback copy of Walt Unsworth's *Everest*. But they knew all the little details about Mallory and Irvine, and Odell who last saw them in 1924; about the subsequent series of British attempts, all unsuccessful; about the Chinese/Tibetan summit by night in 1960, and the first man to climb the Second Step losing both feet from frostbite.

They could talk about the eight Tibetans and one Chinese who took the Chinese flag to the top again in 1975, led once again by Shih Chan-chun; their deputy leader, Phantog, became the second woman summiteer. About Reinhold Messner's oxygenless ascent by the Great Couloir in 1980. About the military-style trinational effort by China, Japan and Nepal, which was covered live on television when ten of the 252-strong team reached the summit in 1988.

They knew about the many deaths, and the statistics for fatal accidents. We passed the nine stone cairns on a mound of moraine on the way in. The inscriptions were in French, Chinese, Tibetan, Nepalese. Among those in English were Marty Hoey, member of the 1982 American North Face expedition, who fell to her death when her harness opened; Peter Boardman and Joe Tasker of the 1982 British North-east Ridge expedition, who died on the same day when they failed to return from a summit attempt; Tony Swierzy, member of a British SAS expedition who died in an avalanche at advance base camp in 1984 . . .

Four of the climbers – Robbie, Dermot, Dawson and Richard – had gone back up to Advance Base. The others were there to greet us, fix us up in tents, and wait patiently for someone to hand over the post. There were some chocolate Everests to unpack, and a scrunched up box of fig-roll biscuits for the Base Camp manager.

Frank Nugent was welcoming, but worried; as the trekkers chatted and I sent copy back to the newspaper in Dublin by modem,[2] he slipped away to the Chinese camp further down the valley. He returned later, almost crying with relief. The missing Chinese and Taiwanese climbers had made contact, having survived a wild night up at 7,700 metres using oxygen and supplies from the Irish second camp. Nugent knew one of them,

Wang Yung Feng of the Chinese Mountaineering Association. It was a sharp reminder of the need to ensure that everyone was safely back before releasing any news. He was keen to talk about the meeting and the likelihood that both he and Dawson would be the summit pair. Originally, he had thought that it might be Dawson and Richard; getting all eight on top seemed to be unrealistic now.

'Put it like this,' he said. 'If we get one up there, it takes the pressure off the rest of us. I might feel a little twinge, but I would still be delighted for all of us if it wasn't me. We're not attacking this mountain. We're taking it sweetly. We're not pushing anyone.'

Forming, storming, norming, performing, mourning: if these were the five stages of group development by Frank's managerial training,[3] which stage was the expedition at? Was it natural that they should seem so relaxed at Base Camp? Why was Mike Barry teaching Aka Raj how to make fresh brown soda bread?

Having read Chris Bonington's account of his 1982 North-east Ridge attempt, I'd been somewhat apprehensive about the reception after my trekking companions had gone. I recalled that when things had got a little rough, Bonington's company had turned on their resident and quite altitude-sick Sunday newspaper journalist.

The real obstacles on such big mountains were often mental rather than physical, Richard O'Neill-Dean had observed back in Dublin. Hugh Ruttledge, leader of the third unsuccessful British attempt in 1933, had written about defects and weaknesses assuming 'strange proportions above the Himalayan snowline'.[4] Even Messner, the superhuman, had admitted to feelings of 'isolation and apprehension and frequent waves of dizziness' which had robbed him of his enthusiasm, his strength and courage to climb.[5]

It seemed such a contrast to the neighbouring Swiss expedition – 'like five green bottles', Dr Kathy Fleming said later on. They had lost their own doctor on the acclimatisation trek when he broke his leg; another member fell ill with adrenal cholic. Morale had taken a tumbling from then on in.

Perhaps it was different up at Advance Base. Leslie Lawrence, who had been there a few days previously, warned us. If we offered him £500, he wouldn't do it again.

Pu Bu, one of the four Tibetans who had 'summited out', came over to visit. The news from his camp was that three of his compatriots had been taken to hospital in Lhasa with frostbite. It was the 28-year-old's third time on the mountain, and the first time to reach the top, according to Khunke who acted as interpreter. The Chinese and Taiwanese were expected to be in a very bad way when they came down.

We met the leader, and the Taiwanese on the way up the glacier, having left for Advance Base that day. The climber had frostbite on his face. He seemed exhausted but cheerful, and was glad of a mug of tepid tea and some Celtic Shortcake biscuits, but we were almost afraid to shake his hand.

A local Tibetan had forecast a period of settled weather before the monsoon, but the conditions on the mountain were deteriorating and it looked as if everyone would be in the second camp when we got there. We took three days – the climbers had been doing

it in two at most – and felt every bootstep on the route up beyond the boulder moraine. This was a geologist's paradise and we were rucksacked intruders on a surreal landscape of fluted, serrated *nieves penitentes* – the Spanish 'snow nuns' or ice pinnacles spilling down the East Rongbuk glacier like shards of crystallised glass.

I had started to keep my own log, drawing on scribbled notes for the reports back to *The Irish Times* later that week:

Sleeping – or trying to sleep – on moving ice,
there were three wild nights of wind and snow,
and frost on the sleeping bags the following
morning. Under a full moon and temperatures of
minus 15°C, one could hear the
glacier groaning and the occasional crack.
Breakfast consisted of half-boiled tea and a
Jacob's biscuit, lunch was a packet of chocolate
eclairs. Backpacks were heavy enough, without
carrying large appetites . . .

Halfway there, we heard the shouts, the whistles,
the singing, the tinkling of 30 bells. A herd of
shaggy, baggy, but sure-footed yaks had been
sent up to transport gear from the departing
Chinese base camp. As the drovers stopped to
cook lunch over yak dung, one animal collapsed
and refused to move. A few kicks, a few whips,
and still it wouldn't budge. It was offered a
bag of meal, and left to its fate.

And then, senses dulled by lack of oxygen, the
mountain itself came into full view – a view that
one doesn't have from Nepal. Throwing out its
white buttresses, it seemed to mock and tease as
it dominated the cloud line. As night fell,
perspective and distance seemed irrelevant. It
was close enough to touch.[6]

It took a while for figures to emerge from the tents, though we were noisy enough approaching the camp. The day was dull, dark; there had been a blizzard an hour before. The climbers seemed tired, drained, almost shy of conversation. They sat around, feet on black bin liners for warmth. The altitude was consuming them. They could not stay up here for too long.

✷ *Chapter 10* ✷

Day 42: refused planning permission for
Camp Two, after a dodgy land decision. We
proceed to further desecrate this sacred
mountain by erecting Camp Three on the
infamous North Coll (*sic*). Our extensive
medical facilities are the toast of the
mountain, and during our stay at Camp Three
we are visited by a French climber with a
broken leg and a Swede with broken English.
We also perform a number of hip replacements
on a group of visiting pensioners from Crumlin.
Meanwhile, the summit beckons . . .

Day 63: The treacherous North Col, perhaps
the most hazardous of all mountain terrains,
has often been compared to St Patrick's Hill
in Cork on a frosty morning . . . [1]

The Phoenix, Ireland's equivalent of *Private Eye*, was clearly enjoying the Irish Everest
expedition coverage. It was bait also for other wits at home. One sketch drew on the film
Alive, the story of the Andean plane crash which was showing in cinemas at the time –
the poor climbers had been hit by food shortages, and had been forced to eat *The Irish
Times* reporter.

It was copy also for a colleague's humorous column. 'More difficult than Everest,
more dangerous than K2, more sublime than the Matterhorn,' Brendan Glacken wrote,
relating the tale of Reginald, Timothy, Jonathan, Tarquin and Joe, who were sponsored
by Safe Harbour Bonding, the Inner Feelings Foundation and Ovaltine to climb 'New
Man Mountain'. Lucky them: they were backed up by a team of 30 powerfully built
female Sherpas – 'without whom,' the author wrote, 'our equipment, never mind our
consciousness, could never have been raised.'

On radio, Leslie Lawrence and Dermot Somers had become the voices of the
expedition. The response from schools was overwhelming, and RTE's Pat Kenny
transmitted regular messages of goodwill. Kenny was particularly taken by the fifth class
of Our Lady of Victories Primary School in the north Dublin suburb of Ballymun. Under
the supervision of their teacher, Brian O'Reilly, the boys had built an eight-foot model
of Everest out of wood, chicken wire and newspaper. They had painted it and marked
out the camps and the route. Later on, they held a base camp dinner in class in solidarity
with the climbers. The menu was lukewarm tea, tuna chunks, pineapple, chapatis and
yaktail soup.

The pressure on the team to succeed was mounting. The newspapers, radio stations,
schools had their dates for the 'weather window' in early May. Within the first few days

(TOP) THE ENTIRE
NORTH-EAST RIDGE,
WITH THE NORTH
RIDGE JOINING FROM
THE RIGHT, JUST
AFTER THE
PROMINENT
SHOULDER OF THE
PINNACLES. (JB)
(BOTTOM) LATE-
NIGHT PARTY AT
BASE CAMP. (JM)

of the month, there were reports of multiple successes from the Nepalese side – 37 people within 24 hours on 10 May. Frank Nugent had grabbed my arm up at Advance Base. Most of the climbers were huddled up there at 6,450 metres while the North Ridge reeled under the impact of bad weather. It must have been like a beach on the south side, to judge by the reports.

'What do you think they'll be saying back home?' he whispered.

There was one simple message that I had to put across in almost every report I sent – location, location, location; yes, the Irish expedition is on the *North* side of Everest! In any other year, there might not have been so much difficulty. However, this was the 40th anniversary of the Hillary/Tenzing climb, and British newspapers were full of reports about the large number of anniversary expeditions, and the environmental degradation on the Nepalese side. It was partly to avoid the south side squalor and relative lack of adventure that the Irish climbers had chosen the dark side of the mountain.

There was substance to the environmental concern. A global report on the state of the world's mountains, published the previous year was not the first to describe the route to Everest base camp in Nepal as decorated with the litter of many nations.[2] Mountains were under severe pressure from such influences as migration, mining, hydro-electric schemes, tourism and climate change, it said. It identified the root cause as poverty, however. It argued that such environments require a high-altitude version of the sustainable development policies gaining ground throughout the developing world.

The expeditions commission of the regulatory international mountaineering body, Union Internationale des Associations d'Alpinisme (UIAA), had already issued regulations on rubbish removal. However, it was worried about the reaction of the Nepalese government which had decided to increase the peak fee on its side of the mountain from 10,000 to 50,000 US dollars and to impose a limit of one expedition per season on each of the three routes to the summit from Nepal.

The UIAA's expeditions commission – of which Joss Lynam had been elected president – felt that this was a mistake. Unless it was complemented by restrictions on trekking in the area, it would hardly touch the pollution problem, and only international or commercial 'heavy-duty' expeditions would be able to afford the fee.

Inevitably, the pre-monsoon season of 1993 would be an exception. All sorts of commemorative events were planned. The Royal Geographical Society had booked Lord Hunt, Hillary and other members of the Mount Everest Foundation for an anniversary lecture in London on 26 May. Its monthly magazine, *Geographical*, was billed as an 'Everest anniversary special'; one advertisement placed by a Scottish distillery offered a limited edition 'Everest 40' blended whisky with some of its own single Highland malt dating back to 1953. A BBC film had George Lowe of the Hunt venture voicing the fear that Everest was becoming the 'greasy pole of Asia'. The romance had died long ago, Jan Morris, the reporter on the Hunt expedition, argued in *The Times*. Queen Elizabeth's coronation in June 1953 had been 'given fire' by that message from the mountain far away. Now, the monarchy was devalued, hundreds had climbed the highest summit.

'Fainter each year are the romantic images of Irvine and Mallory, lost in the mists.'[3] All the more reason for choosing the challenge of the North side . . .

This sort of publicity was far more likely to affect the 21 expeditions at base camp on the Nepalese side; but it was small consolation when it was obvious that they were experiencing better weather. There was particular interest in the heavily financed British venture sponsored by DHL couriers which included Rebecca Stephens, described as a *Financial Times* journalist, who was attempting to be the first British woman on the summit by the South Col. The leader was John Barry, a veteran climber with Northern Irish roots.

It was a little like living in an envelope after the trekkers had left. There was a sense of abandonment as the last of the Land Rovers disappeared in a whirl of dust, bound for Lhasa and sightseeing and a flight over Everest to Kathmandu, and, sadly, taking Rory McKee with them. A skilled and experienced mountaineer, he had not recovered from altitude sickness.

I had brought as many books as I could carry, and even a copy of the morse code for studying at night by the light of a stout white candle bought in Kathmandu. Passing time was not a problem, though; the Base Camp library was good, the conversation was excellent, and there was always a laptop computer battery to be charged by generator, and copy to write.

After I came down from Advance Base, the newspaper was anxious to receive material every day. Fresh snow was still falling, conditions were too unsettled to move. What could I write? There was much sympathy among the climbers – unaware, perhaps, of my reputation in the newsroom for writing weather stories. Every morning I walked down the moraine and studied the mountain.

It began to take on a life. I learned to recognise its weather moods. The summit plume – spindrift in high winds – provided some diversion on clear days when there seemed to be nothing else to identify. It couldn't match the distinctive Irish cloudscape, however; and there were times when I yearned for a glimpse of the sea.

'Dawson, just make sure you get up the bloody mountain when we get Camp Three in, okay?'

'Tony, just make sure you *get* Camp Three in, okay?'

The banter over the radio on the morning of Saturday, 15 May, was a change from the subdued tones of the previous week when wind was high and morale was low. On 14 May, the weather forecast from Bracknell indicated some clearance with winds abating over the next 48 hours. Four climbers, three Nepalese and John Murray and cameras left for the North Col; Murray had recruited the sturdy Jangbu as a technical assistant. The shift was like 'an explosion out of the camp', Frank Nugent had said on the radio.

Dawson had outlined the plan to Leslie. There had been continuing discussions at Advance Base after the meeting of 5 May, when it had been agreed that there would be two summit attempts by two groups of four. Now, four climbers would move up from the North Col to Camp Two – Robbie and Mick, who would carry gear, accompanied by Tony, Richard, Khunke and Dendi. The following day, Tony and Richard would attempt to establish Camp Three, allowing Dawson and Frank to move up there unladen. The leader and his deputy had been selected as the first summit pair.

Dermot Somers was sick. Dr Kathy Fleming, who had spent the last few days up at Camp Colgate, had diagnosed a possible blood clot in his leg, and he had suspected pleurisy. He would have to rest. Somers sounded philosphical about it on the radio. He had no intention of descending: he was no invalid.

Some 12 miles and over a thousand metres below at Base Camp, the optimism was infectious. John Bourke had arrived down from the second camp and so there was lively chat over dinner. Pulling his earlobe and waving his finger, Asha Rai had been talking to Khunke and Dendi on the radio. 'Around 17th, 18th, they will go for the summit, yes.'

'It's incredibly slow, very dispiriting . . . I'm just on the 8,000-metre contour and I'm absolutely buggered.' The hoarse, gasping, Anglo-Irish tones over the radio were unmistakable. Richard O'Neill-Dean should have sounded more cheerful. This was to have been *his* day.

And that of Tony Burke. The pair had been due to make the carry to Camp Three, without oxygen. The forecast was for relatively gentle 15 to 20-knot winds, and both seemed in good shape. Burke had sustained slight frostnip on one hand, but he was the only member of the expedition at that stage to have spent two consecutive nights at 7,600 metres (25,000 feet).

They had set their alarm for 6 a.m., but had slept fitfully in the tent, secured with ropes to the mountainside. It was a 'howling' night; the fabric was hammered like a mainsail head to wind. Come the morning radio call, arranged for 9 a.m., they reported that they were ready to move but that it was too windy. Richard had almost set the tent on fire during the brew-up, and Tony had collapsed in a fit of uncontrollable giggles.

They waited, aware that they were losing valuable time. Responding from Advance Base, Dawson tried to reassure them. The Chinese had described the terrain between the second and third camps as the most exposed. 'It might ease further up.'

At 10 a.m., Khunke and Dendi decided to risk it, and it took Richard and Tony an hour to crawl out of the tent after them, each carrying about 12 kilos of basic gear and food. They were not on oxygen. It would be the last time that anyone would move beyond Camp Two without some oxygen feed.

The sky was clear, but the vexed zephyrs showed no signs of relenting. Mindful of Dawson's comments, they picked their way slowly, clambering over steep broken ground towards an abandoned Chinese camp just 100 metres above. It was to take them a full hour to complete that short journey, pulling on scraps of rope, scrambling around and about boulders and broken rock through the ice and snow.

It was, Richard recalled later, 'crushingly slow'. The ridge marked by towering cliffs was undefined. There was no obvious route ahead, and there were no fixed ropes above the first 50 metres. Despite the wind and the cold, he felt optimistic. He was well insulated and armed with a particularly heavy set of gloves.

His partner was not so happy. Tony Burke indicated that he was in trouble. The three layers of thermal gloves he was wearing did not seem to be sufficient cover for his frostnip. He could see the weather closing in, and had begun to think about his fingers. The tissue was already damaged. Was it worth losing a few digits and jeopardising his career?

He signalled to Richard that he was going to leave his load at the Chinese camp and turn back. It was a psychological blow for both. It looked as if they would not now be able to complete the carry. O'Neill-Dean put in a radio call from the 'peripatetic Camp Two'. It was not quite as exposed as where they had spent the night, he told Somers at Advance Base.

But the daysacks felt incredibly heavy – 'swinging out of your shoulders like a big gorilla', as Robbie Fenlon had described it before. Richard's description was more restrained: 'By heavens, you notice the weight up here!'

Crouched round the radio down at Base Camp, we could sense his disappointment and his concern. As a lone Himalayan griffon played on the thermals and choughs picked on the debris around Aka Raj's makeshift galley, the clouds had begun to gather. Like the occasional little rose finch darting among the rocks, Chomolungma was beginning to taunt us now.

Leslie started up the generator and put a lunchtime call through to the weather forecaster in Bracknell. The satellite images now indicated sustained high winds for the next four to five days. 'By the way,' the voice said cheerfully. 'Climbed your mountain yet?'

Richard decided that he would continue upward for another four to five hours. He had the radio. The wind was unrelenting, murky cloud was moving in, and it started to snow. He wasn't too worried about the welfare of Khunke and Dendi, because he was well aware of their experience. However, he was concerned that they might have turned round, passing him blind in the swirling spindrift, separated by troughs of soft snow.

Dermot Somers was on radio watch at Advance Base, his bad leg stretched out on a stool. Progress was 'murderously slow, very dispiriting', Richard told him.

'You're well able for it,' Dermot responded. Had he been well enough, he would have liked to have done this carry himself. 'You sound very rational, very balanced, in control.'

'That's sage advice,' Richard replied. 'I'll keep going until five o'clock. And Dermot . . . it would have given me the utmost pleasure to have you here with me.'

He met the two Sherpas within the hour, shortly after he had broken out onto a steep snowfield, bordered by a sharp drop to the east. By then, the conditions had worsened considerably. Angry winds drove hail like a sandblast against his face. His hood, his beard, his eyebrows were caked in ice. The slope was so open, so diffuse. With every step, the altitude sapped his strength.

(TOP) THE CHINESE/TAIWANESE/TIBETAN EXPEDITION AT BASE CAMP WITH LESLIE LAWRENCE. FROSTBITE ON THE FACES OF THE CLIMBERS TO THE RIGHT. WANG YUNG FENG (SECOND FROM RIGHT) OWED HIS LIFE TO A NIGHT IN THE IRISH CAMP TWO. ZENG SHU SHENG (CENTRE), JOINT LEADER, IS VICE-PRESIDENT OF THE CHINESE MOUNTAINEERING ASSOCIATION. (FN) (BOTTOM) A HEAVY LOAD JUST ABOVE 8,000 METRES. (FN/DS)

Together, the three men considered their position. There was little daylight left, and Khunke estimated that it would take Richard another three hours to make it to 8,300 metres. He had left a load up there, he thought, while Dendi had stopped about 100 metres short. Richard did not relish the thought of being alone on the mountain with no established camp to shelter in above.

He was relieved to have met them, and he was wiped out. He clipped his rucksack with a karabiner to a scrap of fixed rope protruding from the snow. Someone would find it later and complete the journey to the top camp. For the first time, as he saw the two Nepalese disappearing below, he realised that he was beginning to feel quite cold. His six-foot-eight frame also felt the full force of the drumming wind. As he came off the rock and onto a wider area of shale, he recalled later that it must have been akin to 'trying to walk along an aeroplane wing while in flight'. He feared that he could be blown off the ridge and down into the East Rongbuk glacier. Crouching, crawling, squatting, sliding, he eventually reached Camp Two.

His tent had been battered by the elements. As he ate some plum cake and tried to tidy up the contents, Dendi emerged. He was absolutely spun out. O'Neill-Dean persuaded the Sherpa to carry on with him, down to the North Col.

They made it in a state of near collapse, fighting the storm. It was impossible to stand. Their only option was to allow their weight to be supported laterally by the fixed ropes – 'a sort of Tyrolean traverse across the face of the mountain'. Dendi was having trouble with his eyes. Every 20 yards or so, they sank down into the snow, making it to the camp in the last of the evening light.

Richard met Dawson and Frank coming up the Col the following day. He could not hide his devastation. By the time he reached Advance Base, he was distraught. Stumbling over his words, he broke down and cried, inconsolably. 'That's what Himalayan climbing offers – extremes of sorrow and of triumph,' he said later, when he expressed regret at not having spent a little longer up the mountain.

'The thing that just blew me away was how incredibly slow I was. I found that I was making progress of about 200 metres per hour over the ground. In retrospect, I'm sorry I didn't take one of Tony's oxygen bottles and a mask and put it on at the Chinese camp. I'd probably have done much better, at the cost of using some oxygen at that height on the mountain. It would have meant that my load would have been higher for Dawson and Frank. Every extra hour up there would have been worth it. I can say that now, but then there seemed to be no other decision to take. Yet I had such a crushing sense of disappointment afterwards that it took me some time to deal with that.'

The idea that he might have broken the 8,000-metre contour for the first time in Irish climbing and almost completed the most difficult leg on the summit approach was of little consolation to him. He didn't have his altimeter with him, so the new record in Irish mountaineering could not be confirmed until his rucksack was located. But he had 'tasted' the approach to the summit. 'And it felt quite climbable . . .'[4]

Gao, our interpreter, was to bring us the news at Base Camp from the other side of the mountain. He had heard on the radio that another 17 people had reached the summit from the Nepalese side.

> Yesterday it blew stink round the snout of the
> Rongbuk glacier at 17,000 feet – stink and bin lids,
> prayer flags, stones and pebbles, even an emergency
> toilet tent. For once, the scavenging yellow-billed
> choughs fought shy of the lean-to kitchen where the
> Nepalese cook, Aka Raj, baked brown bread in
> charcoal. Only a lone rose finch clung valiantly
> to a nearby rock.
>   As for the dust, it was ubiquitous: in eyes, hair,
> up sleeves, down socks, on cups, plates, in dinner
> and tea. As it is, food supplies at Base Camp are
> beginning to run low. Four climbers who came down
> to recuperate almost turned back when they heard
> about the diet of tinned tuna and spam. They've
> stayed, for now . . .[5]

Well, even an occasional rockfall from the moraine above Base Camp was worth writing about now. Confidence in the forecasts from Bracknell had been shaken. I had taken on a Pepys mantle, having been assigned the task of log and weather forecast recorder. I never liked being the bearer of bad news. But now it was warning of high winds and unsettled conditions. Stelfox, Nugent and Mike Barry, who had agreed to support them on their summit bid, retreated to Advance Base with Jangbu and John Murray. They would have to defer their plans.

Or abandon them altogether? No one talked of failure yet, but the days were slipping by. On 18 May, Day 63, John Bourke hired the Swiss jeep and went with heavy heart and Gao and Lawang to Passum to order the yaks for departure. The previous day, he and Lawrence had taught the Chinese pair a little Irish; they had also cleaned the Chinese toilet.

Bourke arrived back to find climbers at Base Camp. Richard, Tony and Robbie were down. Within 24 hours, Dermot and Dr Kathy Fleming had also arrived. She was obviously worried about her patient. He had resisted their attempts to have him carried down in case the suspected blood clot went to his heart or lungs with fatal consequences. He walked down instead. Hood up to shield his ravaged features from the wind, he was wraith-like. He doubled up every so often, breaking into a cavernous cough.

So this was what Tibet did to you, he observed a couple of nights later after dinner in the mess tent. Nepal imbued warmth and ease, but the very quality that drew one to Tibet – the stark, spare, harsh and arid landscape – left one a dried-out husk. It was as if life itself was suspended, as if nothing could survive. Even the North Col was like a 'frozen wave'.

The four-stroke generator was beginning to show signs of altitude sickness too. The fax had not been working for days. It was getting harder and harder to shatter the silence in the mornings with the pull start. Fenlon and Lawrence decided to take it to bits.

It was only later that Lawrence found out that a generator suffers from oxygen-deficit too, losing 3 per cent of output for every 1000 above 6,000 feet. In the meantime, they examined it for mechanical faults, lost a vital part, spent an afternoon scratching round in the sand for it and put the machine back together again. I plugged in my laptop to charge up the batteries for a couple of hours. Someone decided to increase the voltage. The computer adaptor blew . . .

The library at Advance Base was getting a little thin; A.S. Byatt would not have been Frank Nugent's first choice. There was a better selection at Base Camp: Patrick McCabe's *The Butcher Boy* was one of the most popular on the reading list. As on previous expeditions involving Dermot Somers, Doris Lessing was much in evidence.

Dermot had seen me with a less than satisfactory book about Nepal. He was right: the rich imagery in Peter Matthiessen's *The Snow Leopard* was far more rewarding. Tony Burke had given Doarjee the loan of his Walkman. He seemed to be quite absorbed by the tale of a mighty cattle raid and the invasion of Ulster in Thomas Kinsella's translation of the Irish epic, the *Táin Bó Cuailgne*.

Frustration might be mounting, but cultural life at Rongbuk was good. There was music: walkman tapes ranging from Burke's Talking Heads collection to Irish traditional music like Buttons and Bows and Mairéad ni Dhómhnaill to the Scottish trad-rock group, Capercaillie. At night, there was the tin whistle, and live and passionate renditions by Somers, a *sean-nós* singer.

There was talk – about Tony's two-year-old daughter on his home-built climbing wall, about Richard's hazardous sea journey in a leaking canoe off the Irish south-east coast. Hot water bottles filled by Aka Raj cooled as we argued into the small hours – about commonage, the constituency of the President of Ireland, Mrs Mary Robinson, the patriarchal society, delinquency in Irish business, human sharks and the state of the west.

The Swiss expedition, which had kindly loaned the Irish Base Camp manager three very comfortable high-back camping chairs, seemed envious. Only three of them remained at Advance Base; another two compatriots, Hans and Christophe, had decided to hang up their ice-axes. They came over to make phone calls home, bearing boxes of chocolate.

The lake had begun to thaw. We could hear the faint sound of running water again. One no longer felt so guilty about asking Aka Raj for a bowl of warm water for a rudimentary wash in the surgery tent. There was never a queue.

It was time to talk, to offer some sort of explanation. Up at Advance Base, Dawson was guarded, cheerful, speaking to me on the radio. Dermot and Leslie were consistently upbeat in the interviews with Pat Kenny on RTE, now taking place on a daily basis. Dermot was finding it difficult, however, to maintain a sense of optimism. One morning

OPPOSITE:

TRUDGING ONTO THE NORTH RIDGE (TOWARDS CAMP TWO). CAMP ONE IS JUST VISIBLE ON THE NORTH COL AT THE FOOT OF THE SOUTH RIDGE OF CHANGTSE. (FN)

we walked over to sit on a rock looking down the valley and he spoke to me at length. His thoughts now were of the reaction. Conditions were obviously better in Nepal, and the relatively windless route on that south side required a weather break of only one day.

'If we were there, we'd get there too,' he said. 'But the satisfaction – of standing on Koreans' shoulders, kicking Canadians, elbowing Portuguese – would be meaningless. We chose the north side because it's the dark side, it's adventurous. Climbers know and appreciate that. What's harsh is that the non-climber judges it solely on the achievement of a summit. We know it's a question of intelligence, commitment, hard work, and the mutual support and co-operation of a small group. We know that is infinitely more important than a summit achieved just any old how.'

For him, there was already a 'summit'. This was his fourth mountaineering expedition, and his best yet in terms of the sense of collective aim. 'No prima donnas, not the faintest hint of egotism among a group of people whose commitment appears to be impeccable.'

Much of this he attributed to the leader, who had displayed 'precision, experience and professionalism' to the 'nth' degree. Dawson had been able to effect ideas without the faintest hint of abrasiveness and without exerting pressure on anyone. The same could be said for his deputy, Frank.

'There's not a blank spot, not a missed beat.'

❋ *Chapter 11* ❋

People blame me for going alone, and I strongly deprecate doing so in dangerous places. But . . . the peaks wear a more solemn aspect, the sun shines with a purer light into the soul, the blue of heaven is more aweful. In fact you are raised upon an atmosphere of emotion; your hardness of heart is melted down to an extent which is impossible when you have companions at your side.

(John Tyndall, 1861)[1]

Day 66. A day of 'trauma and excitement'. Bracknell had given the first good weather forecast in the week. Winds would peak at 50 to 60 knots on 23 May, but a ridge of settled weather was approaching. Shortly after that call, the telephone went dead – Robbie and Leslie were still working on the generator.

Base Camp had become too comfortable. Rucksacks packed on the morning of 23 May, Day 68, Robbie, Tony and Richard ate their two chapatis and some of the last of the fried eggs and strode off in the hot sun, ski poles tipping against the rocks. Within minutes, they had disappeared up the glacial labyrinth.

The mountain above was clear, without even its plume. Its yellow band of limestone had been visible for the last few days. Still wracked by a chest infection and the suspected blood clot in his leg, Dermot was advised to stay behind. If he felt abandoned, it was not for long. A couple of hours later, Richard returned, exhausted and dispirited. He had been suffering from a viral infection that had not cleared; he still had not recovered sensation in his fingers and toes since 16 May.

As he sat down over a cup of hot orange, the light airs carried a familiar cacophony up the valley. 40 yaks, naks and cross-bred zhopkioks sporting red and white tassels, prayer flags and bells had arrived at Base Camp. This was the transport home. A grim reminder that the expedition was on borrowed time.

John Bourke had always been worried about oxygen: would there be enough of it? Would it need to be tried out? They had been using crampons, ice-axes, all sorts of gear for years, but none of the expedition members had climbed on oxygen before.

It was on the second British expedition to Everest in 1922 that George Finch and Geoffrey Bruce had used bottled oxygen for the first time. The four steel cylinders and support frame weighed about 14 kilos, the equipment was cumbersome and the feed could get clogged. The average high-pressure oxygen bottle developed in the former Soviet Union weighed a fraction of that now, and yet even a 3.3-kilo cylinder could feel like half a tonne at altitude.

On the night before they left Base Camp for the last time, Robbie and Tony had planned their effort over the next few days. With Mick Murphy, they had two options: to try for the summit themselves after Dawson and Frank , or to help clear the gear from the ridge as the pair descended. Much would depend on the weather and on the amount of oxygen available. On Richard O'Neill-Dean's advice, the leader and his deputy were seriously considering its use from Camp Two up.

Dawson had been on the radio. The reception was patchy, and so I had taken the VHF handset down to the Chinese toilet. I tried to picture him, crouched over his set in the makeshift mess tent at Camp Colgate. In an early storm, half of that army tent had blown away.

He sounded determinedly cheerful, there was no hint of impatience or despair in his voice. Mr Stelfox, you have spent over a fortnight up at 21,000 feet [6,400 metres] and beyond. Surely you are, by now, feeling pretty ropey? 'No', he replied. 'I feel fine. I think I'm at my personal best.'

Two days later, 20 yaks left for Camp Colgate with their herders. There were four – at most – climbing days left.

It's a lee slope, and it takes 600 very steep metres just to get up on to it. It is such hard work. Every time we go up, clinging to the fixed ropes, we are wading through soft snow. I've done it six, eight, ten times and it is a very unrewarding step.

We've camped on that frozen curve of the wave that is the North Col, plunging 600 metres down on each side. There is such a ferocious amount of noise in the tent, we get battered – but not as battered as the Swiss. The fabric picks up the wind like a drum: it whips and cracks, and there is always the fear that it is going to be shredded around you. At times, it must be like being caught in enemy crossfire. You have an immense sense of your own vulnerability.

In the mornings, you get up and it's calm. You look out over the Tibetan plateau and the Nepalese mountains and it is so icy cold. When you know you are going to be able to go, you shut down that sense of discomfort, that sense of fear.

You learn that the more you fret or worry, the more it escalates. So you tune yourself up, get yourself out and moving and sometimes it is so cold that it feels like wading through nitric acid.

OPPOSITE:

(TOP) SNOW CLOUDS BUILDING BEHIND CHANGTSE. (BOTTOM) CAMP TWO (7,700M) WITH CHANGTSE BEHIND, AND (LEFT TO RIGHT) JANGBU, KHUNKE SHERPA (STANDING) AND DAWSON STELFOX.

> You know that if you do everything
> right and sustain those initial
> responses that you'll make progress.
> There is always a point when you turn around,
> look back, the tents are tiny, and you
> realise that you have left the pain and
> misery behind you.

Leg outstretched, voice rasping, Dermot Somers was talking about the mountain and his experience of carrying loads and camp-setting early on. Compared to the slog up to the North Col, the route from Camp One to Camp Two looked relatively benign, he said.

> But it's a long distance, a long snow slope
> tilting to a ridge. Lacking technical difficulty, it
> induces monotony. It is incredibly wearing, like
> steep plodding. You are carrying a lot of weight.
> That's when the altitude becomes quite serious.
> The thinness of the air at 7,000 metres and
> the burden of 15 kilos on your back defines the
> nature of the ridge. And that combination
> of extraneous physical factors defines reality . . .

Kathy Fleming was still very worried about Somers' condition. She felt that he should be going further down. Apart from the suspected clot in his leg, his chest infection had not cleared. He was very reluctant to leave Base Camp, although he had recognised that he was the cause of some concern.

'I suppose you can't keep blowing your lungs up like a child's balloon and hope to get away with it,' he observed, still stubbornly refusing to depart.

Leslie Lawrence was waving a screwdriver, swapping around transformers to see if he could get my laptop computer's battery to accept a charge. The generator was intransigent. It took an average 60 pulls before it coughed and spluttered and chugged to life. This effort at altitude was shattering. Gao was travelling to Xigatse in the Swiss jeep. There was some serious discussion about whether he should try and buy a replacement.

I spent a lot of time on the telephone, discussing the options with Fiachra O Marcaigh of *The Irish Times* systems team. Would the transformer from a Philips camera work? 'Try it,' he advised, though he sounded doubtful. He had put such effort into setting this system up to work, he had already made many calls to the manufacturer, and now he felt helpless, thousands of miles away. It looked as if I would have to dictate my reports to a copytaker from now on.

The yakmen were intensely curious. As a 'lodger' in Dawson's tent while he was up the mountain, I was having trouble with zips, which kept clogging up with sand. Leslie spent some time on repairs, only to have the yakmen make nought of his efforts when they poked their collective heads in at sunrise each morning.

It was all very friendly, but one did get a bit fed up of being followed to the toilet block. When I rigged up the computer directly to the generator, they were fascinated by the new technology, tiptoeing over to touch the keys, peer at the screen and dart away.

They had been drawing lots all morning to see who would go up with the next herd of yaks to Advance Base. There had been a row over whether there would be enough food for those left behind.

Asha Rai's patience was wearing thin. He had welcomed their arrival at first, and had enjoyed acting as a broker for those who wished to trade their knives and amulets and flints and beads and braids for snow boots, socks and any other expedition gear. They were constantly looking for water from Aka Raj however, and wanted to cook their tsampa or ground meal over the kerosene stove in the mess tent, rather than use their own yak-dung fires.

> Don't stone the choughs. Don't taunt the yaks. Give
> no quarter to the mountain demons. It's that sort of
> atmosphere at Everest Base Camp as we wait anxiously
> for news of movement further up. Conditions look
> good, with summit level winds of a mere 10–15 knots
> expected over the next few days . . . [2]

Even before it was published, the newspaper report was out of date. Day 70, 25 May, and the forecast proved to be horribly wrong. With Bracknell promising settled weather for the next four to five days, Stelfox, Nugent, Barry and Khunke had moved up to Camp Two. Fenlon, Burke, Murphy and Dendi had followed to Camp One, joining John Murray and Jangbu on the col.

Still, spirits were high. Whatever happened, there were only a few days left. That night, as they snuggled in to their 'Deep Sleep' bags, they were in for an unpleasant surprise.

> Very wild and windy night of 24th reported by both
> Camp One and Camp Two. Camp One stayed in tent
> all day. Camp Two battered by winds but these abated
> later, according to Nugent. Bracknell's explanation is
> that a trough passing over is very slow-moving. Winds
> certainly variable. Outlook not good for tomorrow
> according to Stelfox. Snow at all levels. Yaks being
> loaded at Advance Base, co-ordinated by Hayes. Barry
> returned to Advance Base. Swiss abandoned summit
> attempt and returned to Base Camp . . .

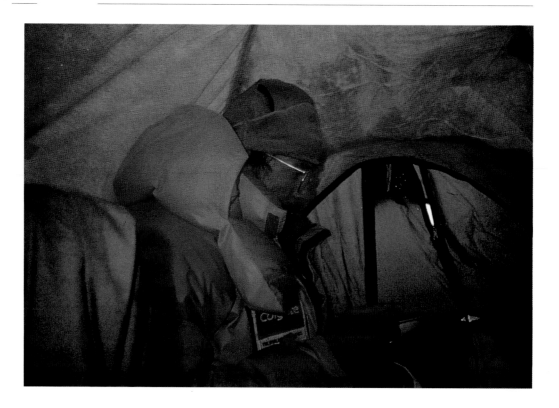

(TOP LEFT) DAWSON
STELFOX AT CAMP
THREE. (FN)
(BOTTOM LEFT)
STORM DAMAGE AT
CHINESE CAMP TWO
(7,800M). (FN)

(TOP) ON THE
SUMMIT RIDGE NEAR
THE FIRST STEP. (DS)
(BOTTOM) FRANK
NUGENT ABOVE
CAMP THREE.
CHANGTSE BEHIND.
(DS)

Mike Barry had had enough. He was coughing 'from his toes up to his throat', he whispered, voice lost somewhere on the ridge on the way down to Advance Base. He was quite matter-of-fact about the choice he had made. It wasn't the wind and the snow and the hole in the tent at Camp Two that had deterred him. It wasn't even his own condition after 15 days at high altitude. 'There just wasn't enough oxygen for all of us, especially if we were going to have to wait for the weather to clear.'

'We had already spent one night, and if I had stayed there wouldn't be enough oxygen to go to the top,' Barry said later. 'If I had stayed, I would have undermined their chances. I had no regrets afterwards – well, it was a bit disappointing but you have to be practical. You can't be whingeing. It would have been wonderful if there had been more oxygen, but then you would also have needed more high altitude porters to carry it.'[3]

At least everyone was still safe and relatively well. It was time to write the expedition epitaph. Even if the weather improved in the next 24 hours, Khunke had no desire to go any further. Stelfox and Nugent would be so exhausted that their chances of getting anywhere would be . . .

John Bourke, whose own secret ambition to get to the North Col had not been fulfilled, refused to countenance failure yet. He gave me his formal quote: 'Far too soon to get into this position.'

Leslie Lawrence also professed himself to being 'very optimistic'. He rooted in his snow boots for a suitable comment: 'In view of the fact that I was on an expedition before with the two climbers who are highest on the mountain at the moment, I believe that if anyone can do it, they can.' He smiled, ever the optimist.

Somers had the unenviable task of talking to Pat Kenny – with some difficulty, due to a jumpy generator. Irish mountaineering expeditions had always been dogged by bad weather, he said. There had been Changtse, with the worst conditions for 60 years, and then Manaslu never really got started. 'We have been promised three good days in one month. And the first turns out to be a disaster . . .'

Marcus from the Swiss expedition called over. The lumbering, chubby mountaineer was the youngest and the most enthusiastic on the 'team', if one could call it that. We had watched his frustration grow, and his lingering hope that perhaps he could be adopted by the Irish climbers. He had reached Camp Two and had no option but to turn back. So he was happy enough with 7,700 metres, he said. For now, at least.

A trekker wandered in: 15 westerners had stayed at the Rongbuk monastery last night, he said. He was a US air force attaché based in Hong Kong. Inevitably, the conversation turned to Tibet. He believed that the new Clinton administration would change US policy towards Tibet, with more emphasis on human rights. He didn't think China would be in a position to give much of a response.

As evening drew in, the wind abated. Night fell. There was hardly a breeze.

Day 71, 26 May, 8 a.m. At Advance Base, Brian Hayes reported a calm morning with a clear sky. Robbie Fenlon was slurping Complan on the North Col and hoping to get moving within the hour. Good news too: Jangbu was going to carry for them to Camp Two after all and Dendi would continue with them then. He and Burke and Murphy planned to carry the minimum of gear and one oxygen bottle each.

Stelfox and Nugent had slept relatively well on oxygen at Camp Two, but a pin had sheered off one regulator or breathing apparatus in the cold. They would leave a radio in a sleeping bag and pick one up further up.

At ten minutes past midday, Stelfox came on the air again. He and Nugent were on the move, and Khunke was about half an hour ahead. It had clouded over, but there was no wind. Snow conditions were reasonable. The oxygen masks were quite hard to get used to. They had located a rucksack on a shred of fixed rope, left there exactly ten days ago by Richard O'Neill-Dean.

One could almost feel the communal sigh of relief up and down the mountain. Could they check their altitude, O'Neill-Dean asked a little tentatively on the Base Camp radio set, as if he didn't really want to know.

'The altimeter isn't handy at the minute,' Stelfox replied. 'I'll talk to Richard later.'

The Bracknell forecast at 1 p.m. indicated that the weather would be 'settled until Saturday or Sunday'. This was Wednesday. All radios were put on standby.

At 4.20 p.m., Stelfox was coughing and calling Advance Base. He and Nugent had made it to 8,300 metres, site for Camp Three, an hour before. It had taken a while to get tents sorted out; the loads left by the two Sherpas on 16 May had had to be carried up and that had taken a good hour, even though they were only 100 metres down. A new Irish altitude record had been set.

Khunke was already on his way back, having left his latest load at a large rock at 8,200 metres. Stripped and tattered tents were a bleak enough greeting to a snowy platform. More snow was falling, but there was no wind, and the sun broke through every now and then. Occasionally, they caught a glimpse of the summit and it 'looked very, very close'.

The stove spluttered to life, and took an hour to heat a pot of water. Dawson promptly spilled it over Frank's boots. It would be 10 p.m. before they managed to cook some food. The weather forecast was good again, and so they planned to move at about three or four o'clock the following morning.

There had been radio calls every hour on the hour up until 8 p.m. Robbie and Tony had arrived at Camp Two and Mick Murphy was behind them. It had been a heavy carry, but both were 'feeling fit'. Dendi, with them, wanted to speak to Asha Rai. He was looking for some Sherpa oxygen – a few packets of cigarettes.

Robbie wanted to speak to Dawson, to find out more details about the Camp Two–Three route. 'No great technical difficulty,' Dawson responded cheerfully. 'It took us six hours, using oxygen the whole way, set at somewhere between 1.5 and 2 on the valve indicator. That took up about three-quarters of a bottle. A lot more fixed ropes than we had expected, and a lot of snow which made it more awkward than anything else. The route is not too hard to find.'

There was a long discussion between Dawson, Dermot and Robbie about the

support team's plan for the following day. Oxygen could be a problem – there might not be enough for three. Frank was emotional. 'Dermot, you know that myself and Dawson are much honoured to be up here.'

The first yak loads arrived down from Advance Base that evening with surplus food: there would be lasagne and instant mash and crackers and cheese for dinner tonight. Somers took to the tin whistle to relieve the tension. He was still under severe pressure to leave for Kathmandu.

As I tramped down to the Chinese toilet before bed, clouds were clinging to the Rongbuk valley, promising snow. There had been a light sprinkling already, marking out the contours of the surrounding hills under the moonlight. For the first time there would be heads in tents at all five camps up the mountain.

Scrabbled round the dacron quallofil-7, high-loft thermal sleeping bag, found the alarm clock, switched it off at 3.45 a.m. It was Thursday, 27 May. Outside the tent, the sky was alive with lights. Stelfox had a better view of it than we had on the 4 a.m. radio call. 'There's a most spectacular lightning storm in Nepal, coming over the Rapiu La!'

He had already been awake for about two hours, and Nugent was brewing up on a troublesome stove. He had taken a look outside, hoarfrost showering down his neck as he moved, dry, sore fingers sticking to the metal zip. It was quite clear, there was no wind, the temperature was minus 30°C. Both felt fairly good, although Nugent's mouth was dry from sleeping on oxygen.

'Well!' Somers responded. 'I must say you both sound remarkably fine, given the fact that you are both sleeping in a tent the size of a raincoat. Take it easy at the start. Drink lots. Don't get too dehydrated whatever you do.'

Someone else was trying to come in. It was a hoarse Mike Barry at Advance Base. 'Just want to wish ye lads the best of luck . . . '

We went back to our tents, resolving to return in two hours. One had to be careful picking one's way across the camp these days, as one slept in the company of yaks. There was a cast over the mountain – more bad weather on the way.

They set off at about 5.15 a.m., as Stelfox recalls, carrying a stove and pot, a rope and two oxygen cylinders each. Night 'swallowed the torch beams':

Plunging up into deep snow, heading for a ramp
we'd spotted the night before, leading through
the rockband that guards access to the crest of
the ridge. But the starless night swallowed up
the torchlight and we wasted time and energy on
dead-end gullies running out against steep rock.
Then . . . what's this? . . . a loop of old rope . . .
pull it out . . . yes, there it goes, up a short

rock step and disappearing into the gully above.
Tug down, seems okay. Jumar on, climb up, push
jumar, sink back and recover . . . start again.

Above, the rock step deep soft snow in the
gully was easy but exhausting. We took turns at
plugging steps up the ridge, reaching it not
long after first light. The storm in Nepal
receded with the darkness, but daylight revealed
threatening clouds over Tibet, a demanding
and difficult ridge in front of us and a
considerable distance to the summit.

It also revealed something else – new mountains,
hidden till now by the bulk of the ridge –
Kanchenjunga glowing in the dawn light away to the
east and Makalu, already far below but impressive
in its shape and beauty.

The ridge started gently, but the complexity of
the First Step was confusing until Richard,
watching through the telescope at Base Camp,
15 miles away, was able to direct us to the right
line. A low traverse around the initial tower,
then up the steep northern flank and back briefly
onto the crest before another tower forced us onto
disconcertingly steep and unprotected slabs. Out
came the rope, six-millimetre kevlar, for the first
time. I led up an awkward ramp to a broad platform
at 8,680 metres, and the remains of the Chinese
tent.

WE ARE NEVER ALONE! CLIMBERS COULD BE
SEEN 15 MILES AWAY. (JM)

To the delight of the curious yakmen, Richard had set up John Bourke's telescope just
back from Base Camp and he was using a hand-held VHF to transmit what he could see.
The next radio contact with Stelfox and Nugent had been just after 8 a.m. They were
'floundering round in deep snow' just short of the ridge below the First Step. The weather
did not look very inviting, but they would 'keep going for a while'. For Nugent, it was
some of the 'softest stuff' he had been through in a long time.

We could make out the legs moving, catch flashes of the down suits in the sunlight,
through the telescope lens. At just after 10 a.m. Dawson reported that the weather had
picked up a bit. He was not quite sure of his position in relation to the First Step. 'Maybe
you can tell us where we are.'

For the next couple of hours, until it clouded over, Richard talked to them,
conveying the details of the route as described to him by New Zealand climbers who had

DAWSON STELFOX ON
THE SUMMIT RIDGE,
JUST BEYOND THE
FIRST STEP,
CHECKING THE
OXYGEN. (FN)

been this way before. At 11 a.m. he was able to tell them that they were at the top of the First Step – where Mallory and Irvine were thought to have disappeared in 1924.

'At the speed you're going, it's better than watching the Grand National!'

Camp Two was empty now. Robbie, Tony, Mick and Dendi had been awake since 5 a.m., breakfasting on complan and a short burst of oyxgen, and leaving for the third camp at around 9 a.m. By noon, Robbie reported that he and Tony were at the Chinese camp at 7,800 metres. Dendi had a bad headache and Mick was about an hour behind. They were keen to support Dawson and Frank in every way they could, but it was becoming obvious that all three climbers would not have enough oxygen. A decision would have to be made fairly soon.

High on the ridge, Frank Nugent was in trouble. He had been enjoying himself early on, kicking and digging through the powder. Now, crampons squealing as they crossed the slabs, he just couldn't catch his breath. Every so often he tore his mask off, gasping for lungfuls of air. Both had set their flow rates identically, but he was forced to turn his dial up. His first bottle was empty after only five hours.

Now he was clawing his way up the slope to the Second Step. His partner was breaking the trail, and Nugent felt that he was slowing him down. His mind was running ahead. What if he was still in difficulty over the difficult rock step, the most technically challenging section of this route? He would need a rope to get back down. They only had one between them. There seemed to be no choice left.

Stelfox was aware of Nugent's discomfort, his fear of losing control on awkward ground:

> It was already obvious that we wouldn't make it
> to the top and back down before running out of
> oxygen and probably daylight; as we moved on
> across a narrow slabby ramp that turned the next
> pinnacle, Frank could see his control slipping
> away. He was constantly forced to remove his
> mask and gasp in the thin harsh air, and finally
> had to take the only option open to him and turn
> back, urging me to carry on without him. He
> stayed to photograph me as I traversed on towards
> the foot of the 60 metre high crag that forms
> the Second Step, the most formidable barrier on
> the ridge and the gateway to the summit. He
> then turned to begin the slow, cautious, descent.

Changtse, Manaslu, Carol, his lads – all sorts of thoughts had passed through Frank's mind. Here he was, on his own, living his own lesson again: 'You have to know when to turn back from a mountain.'

Dawson transmitted the news on the radio at about 1.30 p.m. Frank had turned back. Some 20 minutes before, Mick Murphy had also made a decision. Robbie and Tony had waited for him at the Chinese camp, and he had given the pair his oxygen. They would continue on to 27,000 feet (8,230 metres).

> The Second Step – the psychological as well as the
> physical barrier. Did Mallory and Irvine climb it in
> 1924? Unlikely. Did the Chinese climb it in 1960?
> Almost certainly, and the first man up later lost
> both his feet to frostbite after removing his boots
> to climb the last overhanging crack. The Chinese
> were back in 1975 and neatly avoided a repetition of
> this by carrying up and placing a 20-foot aluminium
> ladder. It's still there, swinging wildly on loose
> rusty pitons.

Reaching the ladder wasn't easy. Stelfox climbed a short, 'chockstoned' and snow-filled gully leading up to a series of ramps that led in turn to the foot of the first rung.

> First bottle nearly empty but turned up full, I
> gasped my way up, one rung at a time, body held
> vertical and pressed flat against the rungs to
> stop the swinging, eyes avoiding the protruding
> and vibrating pegs. End of the ladder, still
> steep.
>   I sweep away the choking powder snow and search
> for holds. A long step out right, a lunge forward
> and I'm up, gasping from an empty bottle and on
> easy ground. Change bottles, mind clears. Radio
> on and talk to Base Camp – Dermot, John, Richard,
> Lorna, Kathy and Leslie huddled round the
> set, eager for news, eager to help, willing me
> on.

If we'd all been willing him on, Somers had been talking him up, while O'Neill-Dean had been marking out his route as best he could. The next obstacle should be a third step, he told Stelfox, marked by a dog tooth of a rock. 'You should should pass this on your right, losing a little height. You should find a little ramp there, about the width of a boot I guess.'

The lone climber had been on two litres of oxygen a minute and now he was turning the dial up to four. 'I've one full bottle left now,' he said. 'That should get me up and down . . . I'm reasonably happy, but not too sure about fit and healthy.'

That was 2.15 p.m. An hour later, Robbie was on air. He and Tony had reached Richard's rucksack, still clipped to an old fixed rope. It was snowing very heavily at that height, and conditions underfoot were 'terrible'.

At 3.40 p.m., Stelfox was 'somewhere on the rocks to the right of the summit snowfield' in 'mid to good Scottish winter conditions'. Somers seized the radio microphone at base.

'You're there. You have it in the bag. Make sure when you get there you don't fall down the other side!'

'It's not in the bag till I get down,' the voice replied. Here was a mind still thinking rationally, clearly, despite the altitude. 'Hopefully my next broadcast will be from the summit.'

Somers took up the tin whistle again, and broke into an air from Carolan.

Frank was stumbling down, still gasping, still tearing at the mask. His rucksack pulled at his shoulders. He had seen it, he had smelt it, and now he was leaving it behind. The first ten steps had been so difficult: there was no adrenaline to bear him down. No relief, no joy, no elation: his mind was numb. There was nothing in reserve. But at least he had daylight, and he wasn't alone. 'Don't look back, don't look back. You don't *need* to be up there . . .'

4.37 p.m. Fenlon to Base Camp. He had just seen Frank Nugent descending the ridge. It was clearing up, there was no wind. 'We're all snow and ropes here, it's pretty hard and very hot.' Somers's thoughts were with his climbing partner.

'Robbie, the rest of your life will be a whole lot easier after this!'

'I don't think so, Dermot!'

Easy ground now – a vast boulder-strewn
plateau. The afternoon closes in, a light
breeze picks up and it begins to snow.
Keeping well down from the ridge to avoid
the cornices, I plod on, searching out
hard snow patches, stumbling into drifted
holes between the rocks. Across the top of
the Great Couloir, eyes straining through
the cloud for the route ahead up the
summit tower. A steep rising traverse
across the upper snowfield, crossing a
vertical wind-slab breakline to a rocky
ridge, out onto more steep slabs. Forced
rightwards, towards the West Ridge, looking
for a break in the steep buttress above. It

(TOP)
A HUNDRED METRES
TO GO. THE
KANGSHUNG FACE
ON THE LEFT, THE
NORTH FACE ON THE
RIGHT. (DS)
(BOTTOM LEFT)
CHINESE LADDER,
1975, ON THE
SECOND STEP.
VERTICAL, UNSTABLE,
WITH DIFFICULT
CLIMBING BELOW
AND ABOVE. (DS)
(BOTTOM RIGHT)
ROBBIE FENLON AND
TONY BURKE AT
7,800 METRES, EN
ROUTE TO CAMP
THREE. (TB)

(TOP) LOOKING DOWN THE KANGSHUNG FACE. (FN)
(BOTTOM LEFT) LATE DESCENT TO CAMP THREE. (DS)
(BOTTOM RIGHT) DEVICES PLACED IN 1992
REASSESSMENT OF EVEREST'S HEIGHT. (DS)

ELECTRONIC COTTAGE AT THE IRISH BASE CAMP. DERMOT SOMERS COMMUNES WITH THE PAT KENNY
RADIO SHOW. IN THE BACKGROUND, A GERMAN QUEUES TO USE THE PHONE. (LL)

stopped snowing, the sun burnt through from
above and the cloud descended into the
valleys. A broad ramp led back left onto
the summit ridge. Steep, with a few short
steps, it was an unexpected last problem
but with the summit close I swarmed up the
steps, clambered out onto the ridge again
and . . . there it was, 200 metres away along
a gentle snow ridge, a minor bump, the
crown overhanging the Kangshung face,
topped by an aluminium pole.

I wandered up the last few yards to the
top, the snow untracked and pristine on
all sides, absorbing the beauty of the
most extensive mountain panorama on earth.
The green jungle and forests of Nepal to
the south contrasting with the brown
rolling barren hills of Tibet. Mountains
from end to end – Kanchenjunga in the far
east, the painful reminder of Manaslu
marking the limit of visibility to the
west, but beyond that the same again all
the way through to the Karakoram and the
Hindu Kush. My eyes wandered around the
Khumbu, picking out Lobuje and Imjatse,
climbed last year with Margaret, Rory
and Niall, and across the border to
Rongbuk, down to Base Camp. Radio on,
make it dramatic . . .

5.07 p.m. 'Everest calling Rongbuk. Come in please, over . . . Dermot, the altimeter is
reading 8,848 metres and I'm sitting on the summit of the world . . .'

Somers sat motionless on the stool by the radio. For a second, there was silence. Then
. . . whoops, shouts, hugs, many, many tears. Asha Rai rushed out of the tent. It was just
half a dozen yakmen, but it seemed as if the whole of the valley had broken into a cheer.

LOOKING DOWN THE NORMAL ROUTE FROM THE SUMMIT OF EVEREST. LHOTSE ON THE LEFT, ALL TRACES
OF ASCENTS FROM NEPAL ERASED BY FRESH SNOW. (DS)

PREVIOUS PAGE:

SUMMIT PANORAMA, 5.30 P.M., 27 MAY 1993. (DS)

❋ *Chapter 12* ❋

I remember constantly glancing back over my shoulder, and once, when after reaching my highest point, I stopped to try and eat some mint cake, I carefully divided it and turned round with one half in my hand. It was almost a shock to find no one to whom to give it.' (Frank Smythe, member of the 1933 Everest expedition.)[1]

Switch the oxygen off . . . Savour it . . . Nothing seems to matter . . . Pity that Frank still has the battery for the video camera . . . Will just have to do with a few photographs instead . . . No other footprints in the snow here.

Lonely? No. Cold? No. Exhausted? No. Detached?

'Yes, detached. Up there somewhere, looking down upon myself.'

Sixty years before, Frank Smythe, a member of the unsuccessful 1933 British Everest expedition had experienced something like it when alone on the mountain; but in his case, he felt he had an invisible partner roped to him, who would catch him if he fell. On his ascent of the east face to South Col route without oxygen in 1988, the British climber Stephen Venables thought that he had a whole party with him on the ledge – climbers, yak herders, even an unknown woman warming his hands.

Hallucinations at altitude are logical, the Austrian Everest solo climber, Reinhold Messner, has said. The greatest difficulty of coping with high altitude is, in his view, the loneliness. 'Humans should not be up there . . . If you are alone, this other person helps you to survive.'[2]

It would be some months before Dawson Stelfox could really describe how he felt as he sat among the flags, the satellite beacons, the snow.[3] The altimeter had actually read 8890 and so he had adjusted it to 8848 metres. Over the radio, it sounded like '884'. After all these months, years of planning, there was an artlessness, a spontaneity, about his summit speech.

> I'm not going to say very much, but it's an honour to be
> sitting up here, and an honour to be given the
> possibility by everyone else in the team. And I'd like to
> think I represent all the other climbers, all the other
> members of the expedition – Irish, Nepalese, Chinese,
> Tibetans, and everybody back home as well . . . You're
> down in the cloud at the moment, I think, I'm up above
> it, and I've got the most magnificent panorama . . .

Frank had been sighted, he was told. I shook my little Walkman, which had been eating up batteries as it taped the day's events.

> I'm really glad that Frank is safe. I only wish he could
> be up here with me . . . It's as much his achievement as

mine, getting up, because there was a lot of teamwork in
the early part of the day and I wouldn't have gone all
the way on my own . . .

If you could please send a message home, especially to
Margaret. The support has been an enormous help
throughout the expedition . . . but also to everybody
back home who helped in so many ways and everybody
out here. It's absolutely magnificent to feel that I'm at
the top of a pyramid of people. I can't really express it
any more, but that'll do for now. I'm on my way down.

He took his photographs, left a flag. Not an Irish tricolour, not a Union Jack – as holder
of both Irish and British passports he would have been entitled to leave both. Unless
Mallory and Irvine had made it – and having seen the Second Step, he doubted it – no
British climber had ever reached the narrow platform and returned safely by the North
Ridge before.

This part had been rehearsed. National flags, national anthems were not in the spirit
of this expedition. He left a pennant, listing the sponsors' names.

Richard O'Neill-Dean had warned early on of the risks on the final ridge. If there was
any wind at all, one might not make it back. The New Zealanders, Whetu, Perry, Curry,
had told him so. The ridge was too narrow and too exposed. Those on oxygen would be
running low. Those without would have a very limited length of time at that altitude
before the body would say 'no'.

For exhausted but elated climbers, descents are often the most hazardous part.
Concentration slips, lethargy tries to take control. At altitude, the body is already dying.
The mind plays tricks. Statistics bear out one climber's description of an unbearable urge
to lie down in the snow.

Stelfox had only four hours of light, at most, to guide him down. He wasn't quite
sure if he would make it to Camp Three, and had arranged with Nugent that he should
leave a stove and pot about two hours before the top camp. It didn't matter that Nugent
forgot. It had been snowing again, erasing his trail. He couldn't even find the empty
oxygen bottle that he had left as a marker at the top of the Second Step:

Down the summit tower with two abseils over the
rock steps. Across the broken spur to the snow
field. Slowly down the windslab break, then with
more abandon, slithering down shallow gullies to
the plateau. Cloud rolled in again and suddenly
I was lost.

OPPOSITE:

THE COMPLEX
SECOND STEP, STILL
A LONG WAY FROM
THE SUMMIT. 'A
TREACHEROUS
TRAVERSE ON SNOW-
COVERED SLABS, AND
STEEP, AWKWARD
CLIMBING' LEADS TO
THE CHINESE
LADDER, JUST
VISIBLE AT THE
CREST OF THE STEP
DIRECTLY BELOW
THE SUMMIT. THERE
IS A BOULDER-
STREWN PLATEAU
(HIDDEN), THEN THE
ROUTE CLIMBS THE
MIDDLE OF THE
FINAL SNOWFIELD,
CROSSING THE
AVALANCHE
BREAKLINE (VISIBLE).
THE ROCKS ON THE
RIGHT ARE
FOLLOWED TO THE
SUMMIT-TOWER,
WITH A SERIES OF
RAMPS AND LEDGES
EMERGING 200
METRES FROM THE
TOP. (DS)

My tracks up were filled by the
afternoon snow. The featureless slope gave way
to the vertical drop of the Second Step. Only
one way down – I had to find the top of the
ladder. I dropped down low . . . no, it couldn't
be here . . . laboriously back up again . . . still
couldn't find it . . . back down again, lower this
time, getting steep . . . hold on, this is serious –
feet sliding and scraping on thinly snow-covered
smooth slabs . . .

Stop. Despair moving in with the fading light.
Calm down . . . Think . . . Remember what it looked
like when you pulled over the top of the step.
Much closer the crest. Back up again, and there,
barely discernible depressions in the fresh
snow – my tracks. Abseil again past the ladder,
back along the traverse and down the narrow
ramp, to the Chinese campsite. Oxygen gone,
three hours to go, darkness closing in. The
radio an invaluable companion – Frank was
safely down at Camp Three, Robbie and Tony
safely up.

Fenlon had seen him at around 6.35 p.m., as he and Burke approached the top camp.
He was able to speak to him 15 minutes later on the radio. With typical understatement,
Stelfox said that he was at the top of the Second Step and had 'got a bit lost there for a
while'. No hint of stress, only relief in his voice. Somers forced him to focus his thoughts:
could he give us some idea of what it is like? For *The Irish Times*?

The reply was cheerful, lucid. 'You'll have to come up here some day and see the view
for yourself.'

7.07 p.m. Fenlon to base again. He was at Camp Three, and he had company.

'This is Frank Nugent here. Reporting that I'm back to Three in one piece.'

Yes, he was feeling a bit knackered, his throat was dry, his explanation was brief. 'I
wasn't getting sufficient oxygen. I got very fatigued. Three hours of step-kicking this
morning in soft snow just wiped me out. I was gasping on the steep bits. But I'm absolutely
thrilled about Dawson. The last thing I wanted was to interfere with his opportunity.

'A terrible snow shower came in just as he was going for the Second Step,' Nugent
continued, still coughing and trying to catch his breath. 'It says an awful lot about
Dawson. For me it doesn't matter. Now I'm getting into a tent that wasn't built for
Brittas Bay . . .'[4]

Stelfox was still struggling down:

Talking concentrated my own mind, forcing me
to think, avoiding automation. Down and round the
First Step and in the last few minutes of
daylight reached the top of the ropes leading
off the ridge, down the steep rock band above
the tents. Headtorch on, plunging down the
morning tracks, grateful now for the deep
trench we had ploughed upwards. The lights
in the tent seemed a long way down.

An old rope lying slack in frozen snow
pulled tight as I abseiled off, sending me
slithering down a heart-stopping six feet.
Off the ropes, down through the deep snow
and suddenly there was Robbie, out to guide
me in and envelop me in warmth, Frank and
Tony brewing up in the tents. The day was
over: 18 hours after leaving, I was back in
Camp Three.

10.43 p.m. A slightly sleepy, confused Tony Burke had been snoozing when he got the
radio call from Base Camp. Had he any news of Stelfox's safe arrival? He came back on
a few minutes later, nonchalant. Yes, he was there all right, 'in the tent with Robbie'.

Fenlon had attempted to go up and meet Stelfox as his torchlight faded. The leader
had waved him back, determined to take those last few steps on his own.

The Irish Embassy, London, 28 May. Tight security. The unthinkable had occurred; the
day before, an Irish head of state had met the British queen. The last comparable meeting
had been four centuries before, when Queen Elizabeth I had met the Irish sea queen,
Granuaile, leader of the O'Malley clan.

There was a sense of satisfaction in the embassy the morning after the half-hour visit
to Buckingham Palace. There was also a sense of relief. Bride Rosney, special adviser to
the President, was just about to gather her papers and start moving when she was called
to the phone.

She had been waiting to hear the news from Tibet. This was *so* sweet. Even as she
spoke and there was a delighted outburst, an Irish official casually asked if she could pass
the butter . . .

Plas-y-Brenin, North Wales, 28 May. Some 80 of the world's leading mountaineers were
taking breakfast at the British National Mountaineering Centre. They were attending a

TONY BURKE AND
ROBBIE FENLON
DESCENDING (28
MAY) FROM THEIR
HIGH POINT ON THE
RIDGE. (DS)

special council meeting of the Union Internationale des Associations d'Alpinisme (UIAA).

Joss Lynam, president of the UIAA expeditions commission, wasn't quite sure if he understood what his wife, Nora, was saying. His neighbour at the table yelled for silence, and relayed the news to the full room. For Lynam, the timing could not have been better. Sir Edmund Hillary and surviving members of the 1953 expedition would congratulate him again at a special 40th anniversary function hosted by the association that night.

In 1953, James Morris of *The Times* had devised a code. Accompanying the Hunt expedition, he knew that his real challenge was to transmit his reports safely from the nearest cable office – in Kathmandu, some 200 miles away. The competition was stiff, and the early dispatches sent by Nepali runners from base camp on the south side had often been intercepted by rivals, either *en route* or at the cable office.

It took an average eight days after writing for his reports to appear in the newspaper. Come the technological revolution, the transmission time has improved dramatically, to the benefit of television and radio. But pity the poor print journalist trying to break a story like that now.

So this might not be 1953, the world might not be holding its breath – but Ireland certainly was. I had worked out my own code for the news editor, John Armstrong, but he had no hint of what was happening because technical difficulties had prevented any transmissions on 26 May. It was only after Stelfox had returned to Camp Three that the generator sprang to life at Base Camp.

There was just one phone call to *The Irish Times*. The newspaper's city edition would be on the streets before a call would get through again.

The first report made an exclusive, and the lead story – above that of the historic Buckingham Palace meeting – in *The Irish Times* of 28 May. The front page photographs were of four people – Stelfox, Nugent, the President and the Queen. Leslie had just started the generator at noon after the long and almost unbearable hours of silence when the phone rang. We raced in to the mess tent, stared at it in disbelief, almost afraid to pick it up. It was Margaret Stelfox at 5 a.m. Irish time.

After that, the phone didn't stop until Lawrence decided to give the generator a bit of a rest. The Great Outdoors shop in Dublin threw a breakfast party; Caroline Doherty ordered in bottles of champagne. Back in Belfast, both Nick Stevenson and Dr Stephen Potts were in bed when they heard. A reporter from BBC Radio Ulster got to Nick first. He was looking for a comment. Nick was delighted – and then realised that he hadn't been told who had got to the top. His real response would come a few days later, when he started to speak to Dawson on the satpack and burst into tears.

The Pat Kenny Show's researcher, Carol Louthe, was contacted on an appalling phone line, and made the best use of her few hours. Friday's programme went on air with the President, still in London, and the Taoiseach, on a trade mission to Kuala Lumpur, giving their reaction.

The President sounded euphoric. She was, she said, very struck by the symbolism of Stelfox's position, as a holder of two passports and as an architect. The team provided 'a very good role model for the island of Ireland', and she had been so impressed by this all-Irish dimension when the climbers had visited Áras an Uachtaráin before leaving Ireland in March. She wanted to invite them all back to her residence again.

The thousands of schoolchildren who had followed the expedition's progress should be inspired by the 'courage, the endurance, the spirit', she continued. And the resilience. It had lifted the whole country, she said. 'I am absolutely delighted with the news.'

Albert Reynolds, the Taoiseach, wanted to say *comhghairdeachas* or congratulations to all the members of the expedition on behalf of Irish people 'throughout the world'.

'I believe somewhere that there's a man from my own constituency, Dermot Somers on the team as well,' he said, unable to resist an opportunity to claim a vote. It got worse. 'I'm a veteran of summits myself and it reminds me of the sort of summit that I had to climb at Edinburgh last December,[5] but I think it's a marvellous achievement for them and everyone is extremely proud.'

Two teabags and a sachet of soup. Such was the lavish breakfast facing Dawson Stelfox, leader and deputy leader of the Irish Everest expedition, in a tiny tent at 27,000 feet or 8,300 metres on Mount Everest yesterday morning. 'We'll be expecting tea at Camp One,' Nugent quipped on the shortwave radio.

'Well, I'm mentally alert, I'm not sure how physically strong I'll be whenever I try to stand up,' said Dawson Stelfox, talking from his sleeping bag '[6]

Everest was still on the front page of *The Irish Times* the following day, while other newspapers, the radio and television on both sides of the border tried to catch up. The tabloid *Daily Star* ran two versions as its lead story on 28 May – one for the Irish and one for the British readership. 'Top of the Mornin' was the headline to the lead in the British editions.

Not only had 'hero mountaineer' Dawson Stelfox raised a glass of Guinness after his ordeal, said the *Star*, but his fellow climbers had difficulty getting the wellingtons to grip at 29,000 feet, and they had planted a row of potatoes instead of a flag on top.[7]

Down at the North Col, a voiceless RTE journalist and Everest film-maker, John Murray, was showing early signs of withdrawal. He had spent much of 27 May in radio silence.

At least it felt like that. He had watched the summit pair's progress while it was clear in the morning through a long lens. It was when Nugent decided to turn back that his radio battery went flat and the cloud moved in to obscure his view. He spent much of the afternoon stripping camera batteries to jury-rig some sort of system, and had just crossed the wires at around 5 p.m. when he heard Stelfox's voice from 29,028 feet.

Five hours later, he heard a voice outside the tent. It was Mick Murphy, with a rucksack full of gear from Camp Two. Together they heard Base Camp talking to Tony Burke, checking to see if Stelfox had returned.

Murphy was in 'mighty spirits'. After he had handed over his two oxygen bottles to Fenlon and Burke at the Chinese camp, his first thought had been to turn back. He wasn't resentful. They had been going faster than him. It seemed that there was no other choice to be made.

But he didn't, he said. He had picked up a couple of discarded oxygen bottles left by the Chinese. 'I kept going till about five o'clock. It was great, except it was stormy all day.' He wasn't sure but he believed that he had made it to 8,200 metres or thereabouts – if so, the sixth climber in the group to cross the 8,000-metre contour.

28 May: 15 hours after Everest had called Rongbuk and Leslie Lawrence had opened up the chocolate and biscuit barrels for the happy yakmen, and Stelfox and Nugent were sleeping fitfully at Camp Three. Fenlon and Burke were trying to keep warm in the second tent. They had no sleeping bags with them, but they had their voluminous down suits. Their packs had borne mere essentials – oxygen cylinders, the tent, a stove, headtorches and ambition. They had done their support work. After a week of sun and chat and chapatis at Base Camp, why not try?

They were on their own now. Dendi had given them all the support he could, until a searing headache had got the better of him and he had descended. They used their rucksacks as mats, curled up their legs, tried to save the oxygen for the next day. They passed what seemed like hours trying to melt snow for a brew and toast their toes on the stove. Every time the water bubbled, someone knocked it over.

They became tetchy, stroppy, didn't eat anything and certainly didn't sleep.

They left at 4.40 a.m. Burke was to wonder afterwards why they didn't leave two hours before. They were surprised at how steep the ridge was. Fixed ropes were missing, there was a lot of soft snow. It felt quite . . . intimidating. Once again, there was a lightning storm over Nepal. As Fenlon recalled later, the dawn was splitting the sky over Tibet, looming black clouds were riven with cracks of blue.

'The shocking thing was the height. On most mountain ranges, you are always looking across something. We were looking down from a ridge the width of a table. It was vertiginous.'

It was, as Fenlon was to write later, a place for 'ghosts and astronauts':

Our headtorches illuminated Tibetan snowflakes –
'falling, like the descent of their last end upon
all the living and the dead'. We passed the point
where I met Dawson hours before. Returning without
oxygen, iced, exhausted, shining.
    The snow steepened. We swung from occasional scraps

(TOP) FROM THE
CREST OF THE
NORTH RIDGE
(7,900M) EN ROUTE
TO CAMP THREE. (FN)
(BOTTOM) DOWN
THE NORTH-EAST
RIDGE – THE
KANGSHUNG FACE
ON THE RIGHT.
SNOW CLOUDS
RISING (28 MAY). (TB)

(TOP) THE
WEATHER WINDOW
CLOSES. TONY BURKE
DESCENDING FROM
CAMP THREE. (FN)
(BOTTOM)
EVACUATION OF
ADVANCE BASE CAMP,
29 MAY. EVEN MORE
SNOW IS ON THE
WAY. (DS)

of rope. The gap between us widened. We struggled
alone in our bubbles of light. Darkness intensifying
the sense of danger.

Five days into the stratosphere, air thinning all
the time. Two bottles of oxygen, each carried from
Advance Base. Above Camp Two, it felt like climbing
uphill underwater with a bad hangover and a heavy
load. Dendi had turned back with a throbbing head,
Mick sacrificed his share of oxygen and the summit
when we realised seven bottles and one tent three
ways equalled failure.

At Camp Three, Tony and I conserving precious
oxygen were slurring lethargic wrecks, cartoon
climbers draining blue from head to toe as heat
gushed from our bodies. A lightning storm discharged
beyond the ridge and the summit pulsed in eerie
silhouette . . .

China-blue dawn leaked into the night sky. Below,
the Himalayas swelled through a blanket of cloud.
The sudden height was shocking. The jolt of a
dreamer's fall, 27,000 feet above sea level.

Then I was on a ridge nearly over and down the
far side. I turned to look for Tony. Urgency pushed
me in the back. Teetering on the roof tiles of the
planet. Alone, Mallory and Irvine a few steps ahead,
Tasker and Boardman just behind. The past lay below,
oxygen saturated.

I waited for Tony at the First Step – a decision
was imminent. If he went on, so would I. Otherwise . . .?
I balanced all, brought all to mind . . . a solo ascent,
the lure of the summit, descent without oxygen. The
forecast had put us in bonus-time, but the weather
window was closing. Tony arrived, his oxygen
draining away.

We were on the last life-raft, air hissing out, the
weather closing in. Beautiful and lethal. We talked to
Dermot and Dawson. An edge of concern. A storm warning.
Tony's bottle was on its last hour.

It was calm and final. We left the ghosts in peace.
Backs to history, we descended into footnotes.[8]

The golden rock was just below the Yellow Band. Tony Burke would remember it. They had no safety net now. He was having difficulty with the oxygen bottle which, he was to conclude, may have been faulty. They were at 8,500 metres, and this was the monsoon.

His partner was on the radio, talking to Stelfox down at Camp Three. Fenlon was feeling fairly good, but Burke barely had enough oxygen to make it to the Second Step and he didn't feel like soloing the mountain.

'Anyway we got one person to the summit so it doesn't really matter . . . Yeah, Dawson, I think I'm on the way down.'

They had *seen* the Kangshung face, Fenlon said later. 'It's just that you know . . . you know that when you turn back on an expedition like that, you are turning back for five, or maybe ten years . . .'

Burke would come back sometime, he promised to himself. He and Robbie. To make that last 300 metres. After K2 . . .

It was snowing heavily now, the weather system was moving up the glacier from the valley below. At Base Camp, Richard O'Neill-Dean was feeding bottled oyxgen to the ailing generator under an umbrella for a last *Irish Times* call. At Advance Base, batteries couldn't be charged on the solar panels, so radio calls would have to be rationed.

10 a.m. at Camp Three and it was easy to forget that four of them were still higher than all but four other mountains on the earth – 'Out of oxygen, out of food, out of gas and out of energy,' Stelfox recalled.

Robbie pulled ahead on the last of his oxygen,
we struggled in his wake, oxygenless, cold and
drained, more often slumped in the snow than
moving, conscious that the ground was still
more than serious enough to punish mistakes
severely, dreading the distance we had to
cover but dreading even more another night
cramped in a small frozen tent without food
and drink.

 Camp Two loomed up in a daze of exhaustion,
but we gasped the dregs of two oxygen bottles
and recovered enough to brew up some drinks.
We added more gear to already overweight
sacks and staggered on, shocked by the amount of
new snow on the ridge. We descended into thick
cloud, up to our thighs in powder and crawled, on
hands and knees, the last, cruel, uphill step into
Camp One. I slumped over the crest to face John
and Jangbu, the last occupants of the camp,
shrouded in snow but determined to complete their

film. Their long vigil on the Col had drained them
both but as we staggered back in they fought the
elements and my tired indifference to record our
relief at being down and my elation at having been
up.

Tony was still some way behind and determined to
stay the night on the Col, but I was determined to
get it over with and headed on down,
down, through fresh avalanches roaring
off the flanks of Changtse and the North-east Ridge,
sweeping down past us so that only the fixed ropes
stopped us being swept off the mountain. Off the
ropes and across the endless snow basin, fixing
on marker flags as targets for rests. Brian and
Mike appeared out of the approaching gloom and
it was an emotional reunion. They took our sacks
and guided us back to camp. With two feet of
fresh snow, the normally innocuous moraines were
transformed into an awkward and confusing maze,
and I stumbled and tripped my way down to Camp
Colgate, following Mike blindly with the blurred
and double vision of complete exhaustion.[9]

PREVIOUS PAGE:
FROM THE NORTH COL.
THE NORTH-EAST
RIDGE/FACE OF
PUMORI (7,161M)
LOOMS ON THE LEFT,
LINGTREN BOTTOM
RIGHT. THE KHUMBU
PEAKS ARE BEHIND.
(JM)

Tony Burke was still up there, but he wasn't really on his own as he curled up in the tent to spend that last night on the Col. He heard the wind, but he thought that he could also hear tent zips opening, closing, and the soft crunch of bootsteps in the snow.

Sixty-nine years before, Noel Odell had been so sure that he had seen them both together on the North Ridge route through a brief parting in the clouds – 'tiny black spots silhouetted on a small snow-crest beneath a rock step'. As the more experienced, it was thought that he would have been asked. Mallory took the younger Irvine instead.

Sixty-nine years later, Tony Burke thought he could hear them. Still on the final climb?

It took him six hours to get down the Col the following day, six hours of swimming in avalanches, grasping for fixed ropes that seemed to disappear. He had a 25-kilo rucksack on his back and he couldn't even find the rope at the top of the Col in the heavy snow. He staggered into Advance Base, shattered and dehydrated, and yet they were waving him on. There was no time now, some gear would have to be left behind . . .

Chapter 13

When the teeth
Of his grip
Attacked,
Did the sounding
Of surrender
Ever fail to come up from
the ice
Before his weight
Bore down;
And the sound of scraping
In the air
Filled the eye
Of a passive northern face.

He has returned:
The face of others lift
To see behind his gaze;
Find the changes
Brought of wisdom
Or a madness
From that place.

(Stephen Potts, Everest, 1993)

Knees. Elbows. Barrels. Heads. Bouncing along the track in the back of a truck, Aka Raj was enjoying this close contact with his Irish friends. An air-dried leg of yak meat came flying across the luggage, hitting me on the back of the neck. Aka Raj grinned – this was one meal he would not have to cook. 'You must hold on, Lola, he whispered. 'Life is very important.'

Wedged between me and the tail-plate, he chatted for most of the way to the village of Passum. Even at the Base Camp party two nights before, he had not been so forthcoming, preferring instead to make sure the hot flasks were filled, weaving and dodging in between the yakmen as they shuffled and sang and danced into the night.

The exodus had been swift after they came down from the mountain – Dendi first on the evening of 29 May, followed by Stelfox, Nugent and Mike Barry and the rest of the expedition within the hour. Somers could not be there to greet them. He had reluctantly agreed to leave for hospital treatment in Kathmandu the previous day.

That evening, Aka Raj and Doarjee conjured up late meals out of dwindling supplies, while poor Dhana had to retreat to his tent with snow blindness. Asha chuckled and rubbed his hands. He had managed to buy a few fresh eggs at the Swiss camp. There was much coughing, laughing, but little drinking. The crate of Chinese beer, the cache of

Sheridan's liqueur, the bottle of Jameson's in Stelfox's tent were kept for the following night when Gao presented the leader and his deputy with the first of many white prayer scarves, and then put on his Roy Orbison sunglasses ('because I am a little nervous,' he said) to sing a couple of numbers from the Chinese top ten.

The next 24 hours passed in a haze of barrel packing and weighing and checking and loading, and more bartering with the persistent yakmen. Leslie Lawrence and John Bourke had already spent a morning scouring the Chinese toilet with kerosene.

Then there was the rubbish – what was left after the yakmen had done their recycling. There would be no fire, as it was best not to offend the gods. It would have to be deposited in the Chinese dump. As it was, Kathy, Leslie and I had almost incurred the wrath of gods, or demons, the day before, when we had been tempted to take a dip in the lake above the glacier. Such was the dismay among the Sherpas that we turned back to the icy river instead to peel off the layers and scrub greasy scalps amid a shower of flaking skin.

The ground still looked parched, but there were traces of green moss now down the valley. In Passum, the mayor and treasurer had prepared yak tea and chang, and wished to present us with prayer scarves as a mark of gratitude. The expedition had agreed to sell the council the generators and some surplus food.

'The poorest village in China,' said Gao, pointing to the little children, hair matted, feet bare, eyes and nose streaming. But Passum had its own television set, and a satellite dish in the village square – gifts from his employer, the Tibet Mountaineering Association. The set was kept in a room of its own as if it was a shrine. Both it and the dish were redundant without power. The mayor hadn't managed to start the generator as we left.

The truck trundled over the Pang La, with Barry, Nugent and Lawrence singing woeful 1960s numbers and Doarjee out of his head with a bottle of beer. The last glimpse of a snow-covered Chomolungma was in the driver's wing mirror, as we sped across the Tibetan dustbowl now on the 'highway' from Lhasa to Nepal. During a yak butter tea stop in Xegar, a group of western interpreters based in Taiwan told that they had been deported from Lhasa after demonstrations there. The US had awarded China special trading status but on condition that it met demands on human rights.

Eyes feasted hungrily on the lush landscape after a night – and another disco, with its own resident break dancer – in Nyalam and a descent to the border at Zhangmu. Lumps in throats after so many weeks, there was a brief farewell to Gao. Lawang had slipped away already. Watching us walk across the Friendship Bridge, Gao sucked at a cigarette, turned and disappeared. Back into China?

The Nepalese staff went shopping with their Chinese FECs in Zhangmu, while there was some hefty hauling and transferring of gear from truck to truck. Aka Raj, Dhana and Doarjee bought track suits and matching runners. Asha bought bed linen, and some gifts for his wife. On the outskirts of Kathmandu, after a day's jolting in Bikram's hired bus, there was an unscheduled stop. Approaching Bhaktapur, a boy wobbled on a bicycle, the

OPPOSITE:

(TOP) AFTER THE ASCENT . . . (JM) (BOTTOM) DR KATHY FLEMING GETS THE PARTY GOING! (JM)

truck swerved and crashed. Asha Rai was in the passenger's seat. He was a little shaken, but no one was hurt.

The fax machine was burning up already in the Hotel Excelsior. The manager, himself a Tibetan, had hung a banner in the Thamel street: 'Congratulations and a warm welcome to the successful Irish Everest expedition group.' There were messages from Government ministers, politicians and councillors on both sides of the Irish border, from the Archbishop of Armagh and the chief of staff of the Defence Forces; the patron, Edmund Hillary; from sponsors, from walkers and climbers and mountain rescue groups, from hundreds of schoolchildren, from all sorts of people associated with the expedition including Anthony O'Brien of the Tibet Support Group who had given all the trekkers little mani stones to bring to the mountain.

His former school, his university, and his architectural colleagues were quick to claim Stelfox as their own. 'It was absolutely fantastic to hear the news that Dentalfloss Smallpox reached the summit,' said one climbing colleague from Queen's University. The vice-chancellor of the college, Dr Gordon Beveridge, was delighted to have 'a Queen's man on top of the world'.

Some of the messages reflected the ambiguous thinking about an Irish expedition which was led by a Belfast and a Dublin man. 'Well done!' read the fax from Michael Ancram, the Northern Ireland Minister for Education and Sport. 'I hope to meet at least some of you on your return home.'

The British Prime Minister, John Major, also fixed the border on the group. The letter from 10 Downing Street was for Mr Stelfox, Esquire, only. 'This is a remarkable achievement in itself but all the more so since you reached it by the North Ridge. And, I understand that you are the first man from Northern Ireland to have reached the summit and the first Briton to have climbed this route.'

Buckingham Palace, by contrast, had no difficulty in recognising the all-island effort. 'Dear Mr Stelfox,' the letter from Her secretary read. 'The Queen has heard of your splendid achievement in becoming the first Irishman to climb Everest, and the first British climber to make the ascent via the North Ridge. Her Majesty has asked me to send you her warm congratulations and good wishes.'

Tiger balm. Joss sticks. Bookshops and bootleg
tapes. After months of isolation under Everest in
Tibet, life this week has been something of a
sensory assault for eight Irish climbers in
Kathmandu.

The monsoon has arrived, the narrow streets are
puddles of mud. The first drops of light rain in
weeks were felt through a half-open bus window on
last week's journey over the border into Nepal . . .[1]

There would be showers, shaving, hair-cutting, clothes-washing, gear-selling, the donation of medical supplies to the Himalayan Rescue Association, and I would send my last despatch from Kathmandu. Steaks would be ordered, there would be talk of *immodium* again.

There would also be a surprise for some of the group: Bob Arnold, one of the trekkers, had sponsored the flights of spouses to Nepal. Planned by Margaret Stelfox, it had been a well-kept secret at Base Camp for some weeks.

There was a hectic social calendar over the few days – a party thrown by the British consul, Brian Money, a dinner with Bikram, and the customary farewell lunch with the Nepalese staff. The bond was firm, though, and Asha was not content to leave it at that. He and Dhana invited us all out to their home one night – a night of music and food and more food and more music and saffron geraniums and prayer scarves. The pair came out to the airport with Bikram to see us off, with Dhana promising to return to his studies and Asha promising to come and visit us next year . . .

As the first flight took off for an overnight stop in Pakistan, the dates for receptions with the President, with the Taoiseach, were already being set. There had been plans for a red carpet, for a jazz band; but though reporters, photographers and hundreds of friends and well-wishers set out for Dublin airport that evening, some of them never got there at all.

The plane which was due to take the group from London almost didn't make it either. It was hit by lightning on the way over. There was a delay until the next, very packed, flight. When we did approach Dublin, eventually, the airport's surroundings resembled a large paddy field. 'So you've reached the summit,' the captain said over the PA. 'I thought we'd reached the estuary,' Frank Nugent quipped.

'Irish monsoon fails to dampen Everest climbers' homecoming' read *The Irish Times* headline the next day.' Everest conquerors swap blizzards for deluge,' read another, describing how cars had to be abandoned on the airport road due to serious flooding. The following month, the Meteorological Service confirmed that Friday, 11 June, was the wettest day on record at lowland weather stations, with over 100 millimetres of rain . . .

Summer *would* come, though – a summer of extreme experience at home. There would be civic receptions and dinners and presentations, turning the Stelfox home into a showroom for various pieces of Irish crystal. A cross-border precedent would be set when the lord mayors of Dublin and Belfast held civic functions in both cities.

Initially, there had been some time lapse in the congratulatory message from Northern Ireland. The authorities had already been embarrassed into action, though, and moves were afoot to give the expedition's success official recognition. The Northern Ireland Department of Education said that a telegram was being sent to Stelfox, while the Sports Council would organise a reception.

However, a proposal that Belfast City Council should host a civic reception would not be discussed until the next meeting on 1 July, it was reported. There was a problem of borders again: Stelfox's home at Dunmurry lay on the boundary of Belfast and Lisburn council areas.

(TOP) AFTER TWO
RIGOROUS MONTHS
ON THE MOUNTAIN,
A CHINESE TRUCK
CLIMBS TOWARDS
BASE CAMP TO
EVACUATE THE
SUCCESSFUL
EXPEDITION. (FN)
(BOTTOM) BACK TO
THE BRIGHT
LIGHTS . . . (JB)

(TOP) THE HIGHEST MONASTERY IN THE WORLD (5,000M), AT THE HEAD OF THE RONGBUK VALLEY, BELOW THE NORTH FACE OF CHOMOLUNGMA (EVEREST). (FN) (BOTTOM, LEFT) BIKRAM NEUPANE AND (BOTTOM RIGHT) MR RAI OF NEPAL TREK HOUSE, KATHMANDU. (DS)

One felt for the Belfast mayor, councillor Reg Empey. He was criticised heavily by some Unionist councillors for travelling to Dublin at the invitation of his Dublin counterpart. A former lord mayor and Democratic Unionist Party councillor, Sammy Wilson, said that he should not be playing 'good neighbours' with Dublin politicians while the Republic's claim to the North, through Articles 2 and 3 of the Irish constitution, remained in place.

'Ludicrous' was Empey's response. 'Only Sammy Wilson could manage to drag Articles 2 and 3 to the summit of Everest.'[2]

The prejudice was not particular to the North: it was just more honestly expressed. Some months later, RTE radio would give airtime to a climber from Cork who planned to be the first Irishman on top of Everest.

'No Irish climber from the south of Ireland has yet put their foot on the summit of Everest and no Irish flag has yet been placed on the world's highest point,' his fundraising letter read.

The fresh breath of air came in newspaper editorials and in public tributes to the symbolism of the effort. A former Northern Irish representative in the Republic's senate, Mr John Robb, identified it in a letter published in *The Irish Times* on 1 June. Ireland's Everest still remained to be conquered, he said, referring to the Northern conflict. 'Whether we approach from north side or south side, let us never lose sight of the summit.'

The Taoiseach, Mr Reynolds, would be presented with an expedition Swiss army knife. Throwing her stately residence open to everyone associated with the effort, the President, Mrs Robinson, would receive a Tibetan mani stone. Both the British Prime Minister and the Northern Secretary would have everyone to dinner in Hillsborough Castle – though the original invitation had been confined to the Northern Irish members only.

Local councils were not found wanting. Kerry County Council awarded 'freedom' status at a function in Tralee which ran into a weekend of climbing and merrymaking at the Barry household and a late night swim in Tralee Bay. There would be another weekend – or two or three – in Donegal, with Ursula MacPherson, director of Gartan Outdoor Education Centre, giving the run of her place to those of us who couldn't bear to go back to work.

Dermot Somers could: within days of his return, he was involved in the aftermath of the court case on interpretative centres in upland areas. It seemed that the Government was determined to push the centres through, in the teeth of environmental opposition. It was profoundly ironic to return from Everest to a row over the wanton destruction of Irish mountains.

The expedition had not dispensed with fundraising either. Crossing Tibet on the journey out, there had been much discussion about giving something back. By the time the last status report had been sent from Kathmandu, agreement had been reached on the details of the Irish Himalayan Trust: to help other Irish mountaineering expeditions and to assist remote mountain communities through funding social and environmental projects.

Richard and Frida O'Neill-Dean left for New Zealand with their two daughters; Tony Burke went home to Wales. Mike Barry began building a house in Kerry, Mick Murphy got a new teaching job in Cork. For some of the others – principally Stelfox, Nugent, Somers, Lawrence and Bourke – life was put on hold, as they undertook an exhaustive, and exhausting, programme of slide shows around the country.

A pub lunch in Dublin, and Frank Nugent is grinning. He hopes to go to Italy with Carol in the spring. Margaret Stelfox is expecting her first child. Dawson has been given a People of the Year award in the Republic, and is on the Queen's New Years Honours List, due for an MBE. During the televised presentation of the People of the Year award by the Taoiseach in Dublin, the climber had made a remarkable speech – political in content yet sensitive in tone – at a time when the Irish and British governments were involved in a new political initiative for Northern Ireland.

Frank talks of the expedition, the plans, the fact that everyone came home with fingers and toes. Stelfox himself had said that it was 'never a death or glory thing'. He talks about the impact on Irish mountaineering, and about the slide-show trail. One of the most recent had been in a prison.

Reliving that experience – what is it like? Frank laughs, makes light of his own speculation about faulty oxygen bottles. 'I suppose I know that I don't have to climb Everest . . . I'm never going to give my life for it. Being there was enough.'

And the mountain is still there now . . .

DETAIL, RONGBUK
MONASTERY
(5,000M). (JM)

MANI STONES INSCRIBED 'OM MANI PADME HUM': ÓMÓS DON SEÓD SA LEÓITEÓG – HAIL TO THE JEWEL IN THE LOTUS. (JB)

✳ *Epilogue* ✳

'Because it is there' explains nothing. Why were *we* there?

Some climbers have the souls of soldiers – their mountains are fortresses under attack. Others are akin to poets – their peaks appear like temples. We fall between.

One evening, as if routed by a bomb-alert, we tumbled out of Base Camp onto the moraine and craned towards the mountain we knew so well. Everest was transformed; in its place we beheld – Chomolungma.

There is no proof of this . . .

The upper half of the mountain was mantled in magnificence, a golden Alpenglow so intense, and yet so frail, that it must burn out instantly – and yet it endured, intensified, as if some essence of the mountain was burning and increasing as it burned.

It was like a surge of radiance that inflames the nerves and shakes the parchment of the body with an ecstasy that must turn to aching ash –

For a few moments the wheel of eternity turned in that place, and we stood transfixed on the prehistoric glacier where a dislodged pebble rolled through multi-millennia to land beside a space-age boot.

The myth of the mountain was manifest, as if we had shuttled in time and glimpsed its nascent geology glowing with the heat of creation.

And then it was gone, sunset quenched in the dusk, as the cold weight of time closed around the ancient shadow.

We stumbled on the glacier, dragging our wings, like moths robbed of a luminous vision.

There is no photo of this, as if it never happened; miracles occur in the heart.

Dermot Somers

OPPOSITE:

CAMP ONE (7,000M)
IN THE GRIP OF A
CORROSIVE FROST.

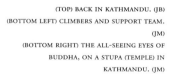

(TOP) BACK IN KATHMANDU. (JB)
(BOTTOM LEFT) CLIMBERS AND SUPPORT TEAM.
(JM)
(BOTTOM RIGHT) THE ALL-SEEING EYES OF
BUDDHA, ON A STUPA (TEMPLE) IN
KATHMANDU. (JM)

(TOP) BASE CAMP MANAGER, LESLIE LAWRENCE, VISITS THE MEMORIAL CAIRNS TO
THOSE WHO DIED ON THE NORTH SIDE OF EVEREST. MALLORY AND IRVINE ARE
REMEMBERED HERE IN SIGHT OF THE RIDGE WHERE THEY DISAPPEARED IN 1924. (JB)
(BOTTOM LEFT) WOOD CARVING IS A TRADITIONAL ART IN THE VALLEY OF
KATHMANDU. (JM)
(BOTTOM RIGHT) MORE ALL-SEEING EYES . . .

✳ *Glossary* ✳

ABSEIL: descent of a rock face by sliding down a rope, usually doubled.

ARÊTE: A sharp ridge or rocky, narrow edge on a mountain.

BERGSCHRUND: a crevasse separating the head of a glacier or snowfield from a mountain face.

COULOIR: a gully.

CRAMPON: lightweight alloy frame with spikes which is strapped to mountaineering boots to allow for grip on ice.

FIXED ROPE: rope fixing in big mountains is laborious, but means that a route need only be 'climbed' once. It allows for quick and safe passage between camps.

JUMAR: a metal clamp used for securing the climber to a fixed rope. It can be slid up the rope, but locks into position under pressure.

KARABINER: A snap-link clip securing the climber or rope to an anchor or a runner.

PEAK FEE: Fees paid to the government of the relevant country for permission to climb a Himalayan peak. Some mountain routes are booked many years in advance.

SERAC: a cube-shaped mass or pillar of ice into which a glacier breaks on a steep incline.

SIRDAR: Nepalese word for foreman of a group of guides or porters.

Appendices

The members of the first Irish Everest Expedition, 1993, were:

CLIMBERS

LEADER Dawson Stelfox, *Belfast*

DEPUTY Frank Nugent, *Dublin*

CLIMBERS Mike Barry, *Tralee, Co. Kerry*

Tony Burke, *Dublin/Cardiff, Wales*

Robbie Fenlon, *Dublin/Donegal*

Mick Murphy, *Cork*

Richard O'Neill-Dean, *Meath/New Zealand*

Dermot Somers, *Roscommon/Wicklow*

SUPPORT

TREASURER John Bourke

BASE CAMP Leslie Lawrence, *Dublin*

Nick Stevenson, *Belfast*

DOCTORS Kathryn Fleming, *Belfast*

Stephen Potts, *Belfast*

AGENT Bikram Neupane, *Nepal Trek House*

SIRDAR Asha Rai, *Nepal Trek House*

HIGH-ALTITUDE PORTERS Khunke Sherpa

Jangbu Sherpa

COOKS Dendi Sherpa, Aka Raj, Dhana Rai

Doarjee Sherpa

FILM CREW John Murray, *Dublin*

Brian Hayes, *Kerry/Dublin*

Rory McKee, *Down*

MEDIA Lorna Siggins, *The Irish Times*

LIAISON

Tibet Mountaineering Association

OFFICER La Wang, Tibet

INTERPRETER Gao Lang Zi, *Tibet*

(TOP) BASE CAMP UNDER THE SNOUT OF THE
RONGBUK GLACIER. (LS)
(BOTTOM LEFT) PRAYERS BLOWN ON THE WIND.
(JM)
(BOTTOM RIGHT) HINDU IMAGE, DURBAR
SQUARE, KATHMANDU. (JM)

IRISH MOUNT EVEREST TREKS 1993

TREK LEADERS	TREK 1	TREK 2	TREK 3
Damien Cashin	Bob Arnold	Moya Bourke	Terence Bannon
Tom Clear	Mairín Begley	Maurice Burris	Terry Barrett
MANAGER Caroline	Cathy Buchanan	Valerie Burris	Seamus Brady
Doherty, The Great	Sara Duff	Raymond Field	Una Coghlan
Outdoors	Marcella Dunne	Paul Hussey	Martin Dunn
	Karl Flynn	Lesley Lawrence	Brendan Henshaw
	Robert Jocelyn	Noel Masterson	Anne Marie Hughes
	Aidan Lawlor	John Monaghan	David Irwin
	Alan Sanfey	Andrew Moynihan	Jessica Kavanagh
	Hanna Shields	Mark Kellett	Morrough Kavanagh
	Susan Spruce	Eoin Thynne	Frank O'Reilly
	Rodney Teck		Phil Ormrod
			Neil Warnock

CHAPTER 1

1. *Everest Reconnaissance*, Charles Howard-Bury and George Leigh Mallory; introduction by Marian Keaney (Hodder & Stoughton, 1991).

Although Everest had been identified as the world's highest mountain in sightings made by the India Survey in 1849, and had been named a few years later in honour of Colonel George Everest, former surveyor general of India, lack of finance and an uncertain political situation in Tibet had precluded further investigation. In 1920 the Royal Geographical Society and the Alpine Club were keen to pursue it.

2. Ibid.

3. *Everest: The Best Writing and Pictures from Seventy Years of Human Endeavour*, edited by Peter Gillman. (Little, Brown & Co).

4. *People in High Places: Approaches to Tibet*, by Audrey Salkeld. (Jonathan Cape, 1991). Interestingly, Mallory did not discover the most straightforward approach; instead of following the east Rongbuk glacier, he made a roundabout journey of some 40 miles to the north and east.

5. *The Irish Times*, 16 October 1981, interview with John Stanley.

6. Interview with the author, 20 October 1993.

CHAPTER 2

1. *The Irish Climber 1984*, edited by Clare Torrans (Federation of Mountaineering Clubs of Ireland).

2. Stelfox was expedition treasurer – a responsibility which, the expedition report noted, was 'not his forte'.

3. *Irish Mountain Log* No. 13, Winter 1989.

4. *The Sunday Tribune*, 14 April 1991.

CHAPTER 3

1. *Irish Mountain Log* No. 19, Summer 1991.

2. *The Sunday Tribune*, 21 April 1991.

3. *The Sunday Tribune*, 28 April 1991.

4. *The Sunday Tribune*, 12 May 1991.

5. Ibid.

6. *Irish Mountain Log* No. 20, Autumn 1991.

7. *The Sunday Tribune*, 21 April 1991.

CHAPTER 4

1. *Rock Climbing Guide to Dalkey*, edited by Howard Hebblethwaite and Colm O Cofaigh (seventh issue, Mountaineering Council of Ireland, 1991).

2. Ibid.

3. Up to March 1994, there were some 60 ascents of Everest without oxygen, according to Xavier Eguskitza, who has compiled the international statistics. (Ref: *Everest*, edited by Peter Gillman (Little, Brown, 1993). Oxygenless ascents are classified as those achieved without using artificial oxygen at all – at any stage of ascent or descent. The majority of these have been by southern routes. The first oxygenless ascents by the North Ridge route were in 1990, by six members of an international peace climb. No westerner has come near the record set by the Nepalese Sherpa Ang Rita. Not only had he made eight ascents of Everest by 1994, but all of them were without oxygen.

CHAPTER 5

1. Elizabeth Hawley, *The Independent* (Nepal), 3 March 1993.

CHAPTER 8

1. *People in High Places* by Audrey Salkeld, pp. 56-57.

2. 'Chomolungma' by Dawson Stelfox in *Mount Everest First Irish Ascent '93: Expedition Report*.

CHAPTER 9:

1. *The Irish Times*, 8 May 1993.

2. To the delight of *The Irish Times* system team, particularly Joe Breen and Fiachra Ó Marcaigh who had put in so much effort to ensure the modem would work on the satellite link.

3. Quoted by Frank Nugent from *Developmental Sequence in Groups* by B. Tuckman.

4. *Everest 1933* by Hugh Ruttledge (Hodder & Stoughton, 1934).

5. *All Fourteen Eight-Thousanders* by Reinhold Messner (Cloudcap, 1988).

6. *The Irish Times*, 15 May 1993.

CHAPTER 10

1. *The Phoenix*, 21 May 1993.

2. *The State of the World's Mountains: a Global Report*, edited by Peter B. Stone (Zed Books, 1992).

3. *The Times*, 15 May 1993.

4. Within a week of the report of O'Neill-Dean's achievement, a letter from Mrs Gay Taylor of Dublin appeared in *The Irish Times* claiming the record for the first Irishman to climb over 8,000 metres (or 26,000 feet) on behalf of Dr Terence Taylor. He had reached 26,420 feet in May 1992 while with a British Telecom expedition on Makalu. This record was confirmed by Joss Lynam in *Irish Mountain Log*, No. 27, Summer 1993.

5. *The Irish Times*, 21 May 1993.

CHAPTER 11

1. 'John Tyndall, 1820-1893, Ireland's first great mountaineer', by Joss Lynam, in *Irish Mountain Log*, No. 29, Winter 1993.

2. *The Irish Times*, 25 May 1993.

3. Mike Barry in interview with the author, February 1994. He confirmed that there were enough regulators. They had a manifold which would have allowed two of them to feed off one oxygen bottle.

CHAPTER 12

1. 'The Second Assault' by Frank S. Smythe in *Everest 1933* by Hugh Ruttledge.

2. Reinhold Messner speaking on BBC Radio 4, April 1994.

3. Stelfox in interview with the author, November 1993.

4. Brittas Bay is a popular summer beach resort on the sheltered Irish east coast county of Wicklow.

5. The European Union summit in Edinburgh, Scotland, December 1992.

6. *The Irish Times*, 29 May 1993.

7. *The Daily Star*, British edition, 29 May 1993.

8. 'Headlines and Footnotes' by Robbie Fenlon in *AFAS News* No. 10, Autumn/Winter 1993.

9. 'Chomolungma' by Dawson Stelfox in *Mount Everest First Irish Ascent '93: Expedition Report*.

CHAPTER 13

1. *The Irish Times*, 12 June 1993.

OVERLEAF:

SUNSET FROM CAMP THREE. PUMORI, LEFT OF CENTRE. (DS)